Improve Your WORD POWER

Clifford Sawhney

Published by:

V&S PUBLISHERS

F-2/16, Ansari road, Daryaganj, New Delhi-110002
☎ 23240026, 23240027 • *Fax:* 011-23240028
Email: info@vspublishers.com • *Website:* www.vspublishers.com

Branch : Hyderabad
5-1-707/1, Brij Bhawan (Beside Central Bank of India Lane)
Bank Street, Koti Hyderabad - 500 095
☎ 040-24737290
E-mail: vspublishershyd@gmail.com

Distributors :

▶ **Pustak Mahal®**, Delhi
J-3/16, Daryaganj, New Delhi-110002
☎ 23276539, 23272783, 23272784 • *Fax:* 011-23260518
E-mail: sales@pustakmahal.com • *Website:* www.pustakmahal.com
Bengaluru: ☎ 080-22234025 • *Telefax:* 22240209
Patna: ☎ 0612-3294193 • *Telefax:* 0612-2302719

▶ **PM Publication**
- 10-B, Netaji Subhash Marg, Daryaganj, New Delhi-110002
  ☎ 23268292, 23268293, 23279900 • *Fax:* 011-23280567
- 6686, Khari Baoli, Delhi-110006
  ☎ 23944314, 23911979

▶ **Unicorn Books**
Mumbai :
23-25, Zaoba Wadi (Opp. VIP Showroom), Thakurdwar, Mumbai-400002
☎ 22010941 • *Telefax:* 022-22053387

© **Copyright: V&S Publishers**
ISBN 978-93-813840-2-2
Edition 2011

The Copyright of this book, as well as all matter contained herein (including illustrations) rests with the Publishers. No person shall copy the name of the book, its title design, matter and illustrations in any form and in any language, totally or partially or in any distorted form. Anybody doing so shall face legal action and will be responsible for damages.

Printed at : Param Offsetters, Okhla, New Delhi-110020

Dedication

To my wife, Monika, for her support and understanding through thick and thin... My seven-year-old daughter, Tanya, for adding sugar and spice to our lives... And to my two-year-old son, Aryan, for all the mischief and mayhem in our everyday existence...

Acknowledgements

This book was possible thanks to the dozens of books and websites already existing on the subject. While it is not possible to individually acknowledge all the sources, the author is indebted to all these efforts, without which this book would not have seen the light of day.

Contents

Synonyms and Antonyms	9
Mastering Punctuation	25
Homonyms	37
Foreign Words in English	63
Slang and Rhyming Language	71
Eponyms or Name Words	83
The Magic of Newborn Words	99
The Portmanteau Combos	104
Talking Numbers	107
Commonly Confused Words	119
Revealing Prefixes	141
Telltale Suffixes	152
Group Terms	162
Some Commonly Misspelled Words	175
Reticent Abbreviations	199
A Few Words About Words	216
The Exploding World of SMS Words	218

Synonyms and Antonyms

Reading synonyms and antonyms can be fun, while expanding your vocabulary at the same time. A *synonym* is a *word or phrase that means the same as another word or phrase in the same language*, as for instance, *depart* and *leave*. And an *antonym* is *a word that is opposite in meaning to a particular word*, for instance, *arrive* is the antonym of *depart*. Whilst browsing through synonyms and antonyms, at one fell swoop you will pick up many words with the same or a related meaning.

So enjoy this list of synonyms and antonyms and then get around to preparing your own list of S&As. There is no more enjoyable way of boosting your word power.

Abbreviate: Shorten (a word, phrase or text)

Synonym: Abridge, condense, contract, reduce, decrease, lessen, curtail, minimise, shorten, trim.
Antonym: Elongate, elaborate, lengthen, stretch, maximise, enhance, increase, add.

Acknowledge: *1. To accept or admit the existence or truth of. 2. Confirm receiving something or express gratitude for. 3. Greet with words or gestures.*

Synonym: Accept, own up, concede, confess, avow, admit, grant, allow, sanction, ratify, approve.
Antonym: Disown, disclaim, forswear, disavow, deny, dispute, challenge, oppose, disapprove.

Apparent: *1. Readily perceived or understood. 2. Seeming real or true.*

Synonym: Evident, distinct, obvious, manifest, visible, seeming, ostensible, plain, clear, discernible, observable, detectable, noticeable, conspicuous, definite, clear-cut, unmistakable, glaring.

Antonym: Obscure, indistinct, latent, veiled, unclear, imperceptible, invisible, indiscernible, inconspicuous, vague, blurred, hazy, misty, foggy, hidden, obscured, submerged.

Attest: *1. Provide or serve as clear evidence of. 2. Declare that something exists.*

Synonym: Confirm, authenticate, verify, establish, prove, demonstrate, affirm, substantiate, validate, certify, vindicate, justify, corroborate.

Antonym: Doubt, suspect, negate, damage, undermine, expose, weaken, refute, rebut, contradict, disprove, contraindicate.

****

B

Blame: To place the responsibility for a fault or wrongdoing to.

Synonym: Slander, censure, libel, reproach, implicate, incriminate, castigate, upbraid, criticise, chastise, scold, chide, rebuke, reprimand, reprehend, denigrate, disapprove, deplore, lament, disparage, belittle, run down.

Antonym: Appreciate, applaud, exalt, extol, praise, acclaim, commend, compliment, cheer.

Boost: *Help or encourage to increase or improve.*

Synonym: Aid, promote, encourage, swell, reinforce, bolster, buttress, add, accrue.

Antonym: Discourage, hinder, hamper, reduce, diminish, deduct, subtract, shrink, retrench, lessen, dwindle, slacken, wane, decelerate, slide, slump.

Brutal: *1. Very violent. 2. Making no attempt to disguise unpleasantness.*

Synonym: Inhuman, savage, barbarous, violent, fierce, ferocious, murderous, bloodthirsty, aggressive, belligerent, rowdy.

Antonym: Compassionate, merciful, humane, moderate, sensible, restrained, mild, gentle.

****

C

Cancel: *1. To put off (a planned event). 2. Neutralise or negate. 3. Delete.*

Synonym: Annul, revoke, obliterate, nullify, invalidate, negate, veto, deny, refuse, reject, repudiate, renounce, abjure, abnegate, abrogate, repeal.

Antonym: Confirm, endorse, corroborate, affirm, assert, admit, confess, avow, second, support, back, commit.

Careful: Taking care to avoid any mishap or harm.

Synonym: Cautious, meticulous, conscientious, considerate, attentive, solicitous, prudent, circumspect, judicious, wary, thorough, meticulous, scrupulous, accurate, rigorous, painstaking, methodical.

Antonym: Careless, sloppy, slipshod, negligent, forgetful, inattentive, neglectful, casual, lax, lackadaisical, slack, slovenly, reckless, imprudent, indiscreet, impetuous.

Cunning: Expert in achieving one's objectives through deceit, lies or evasion.

Synonym: Crafty, clever, artful, ingenious, deceitful, unscrupulous, dishonest, sly, wily, tricky, duplicitous, treacherous, perfidious, fraudulent, shifty, furtive, deceptive.

Antonym: Naïve, innocent, artless, truthful, veracious, upright, candid, sincere, open, frank, forthright, direct, ingenuous, guileless.

****

Defeat: *1. To win a victory over. 2. Prevent (something) from being done.*

Synonym: Overcome, rout, outwit, lose, frustrate, failure, downfall, overthrow.

Antonym: Win, victory, triumph, success, achievement, attainment, conquest, accomplishment.

Deny: *1. To refuse to admit the truth or existence of. 2. Refuse to give (something).*

Synonym: Refute, renounce, abjure, negate, repudiate, challenge, expose, rebut, invalidate, condemn, denounce.

Antonym: Endorse, verify, comply, demonstrate, show, prove, affirm, justify, explain, elucidate, illustrate, corroborate, substantiate, vindicate.

Destroy: *To put an end to the existence of (something).*

Synonym: Eradicate, exterminate, wreck, annihilate, obliterate, delete, expunge, nullify, erase, abolish, liquidate, extirpate, decimate, massacre, slaughter, butcher, devour, devastate.

Antonym: Restore, create, build, save, preserve, maintain, conserve, protect.

****

E

Eager: *1. Strongly wanting to do or have. 2. Keenly expectant or interested.*

Synonym: Desirous, enthusiastic, zealous, expectant, agog, inclined.

Antonym: Cool, indifferent, apathetic, uninterested, unwilling, reluctant, disinclined, loath, averse, unenthusiastic, uncooperative.

Endorse: *Declare one's open support for.*

Synonym: Confirm, support, accredit, buttress, assent, consent, concur, agree, accept, accede, grant, allow, acknowledge, sanction, ratify, approve, welcome, back, second, applaud.

Antonym: Reject, condemn, censure, discredit, dispute, challenge, oppose, defy, deny, negate, reject, repudiate, disapprove.

Evident: *Clear, obvious.*

Synonym: Obvious, manifest, distinct, overt, visible, discernible, perceptible, plain, clear, observable, detectable, noticeable, conspicuous, definite, unmistakable, clear-cut.

Antonym: Obscure, secret, covert, hidden, invisible, unseen, imperceptible, faint, vague, unclear, blurred, indistinct, indiscernible, unrecognisable, inconspicuous.

****

Famous: Well known, known by many people.

Synonym: Noted, renowned, well known, prominent.
Antonym: Unknown, obscure, insignificant, inconsequential.

Faraway: At a distance in space or time.

Synonym: Distant, remote, far-off, far-flung, outlying.
Antonym: Close-by, near, nearby, adjoining, local, neighbouring.

Frail: *1. Weak and delicate. 2. Easily damaged or broken.*

Synonym: Weak, feeble, infirm, delicate, vulnerable, senile, debilitated, ineffectual, unfit, impotent.
Antonym: Strong, robust, healthy, vigorous, powerful, steely, potent, virile, fit, sound, energetic, dynamic, athletic, able-bodied, muscular, brawny.

****

Gallant: *1. Brave and heroic. 2. Charming and chivalrous.*

Synonym: Brave, daring, heroic, chivalrous, courageous, bold, audacious, plucky, dashing, spirited, spunky, intrepid, fearless, dauntless, doughty, stout-hearted, manly, unflinching, macho.
Antonym: Cowardly, dastardly, craven, pusillanimous, faint-hearted, timid, lily-livered, gutless, spineless, defeatist.

Glorify: *1. Praise and worship. 2. Describe something as admirable, especially without justification.*

Synonym: Praise, extol, exalt, deify, acclaim, esteem, honour, lionise, revere, beatify, canonise, deify, worship.
Antonym: Abuse, condemn, rundown, tarnish, disparage, denigrate, smear, expose, dishonour, disgrace, discredit, blot, sully, mar, taint.

Glitter: *1. Shine with a bright, reflected light. 2. Impressively successful.*

Synonym: Shine, shimmer, sparkle, twinkle, gleam, glow, dazzle.
Antonym: Dull, dark, dim, gloomy, murky, dingy, smoky, shadowy.

****

Happy: Feeling or displaying pleasure and contentment.

Synonym: Joyful, content, cheerful, jolly, jovial, glad, delighted, pleased, satisfied, thrilled, excited, ecstatic, elated, merry, cheery.

Antonym: Sad, depressed, unhappy, sorrowful, melancholy, disconsolate, gloomy, woeful, wretched, miserable, despairing, dejected, despondent, distraught, anguished, troubled, worried, anxious, vexed, fretful.

Harsh: *1. Rough or jarring to the senses. 2. Cruel or severe.*

Synonym: Grim, cruel, jarring, severe, raucous, strident, shrill, cacophonous, drastic, draconian, dissonant, rigorous, extreme, oppressive.

Antonym: Soft, mild, gentle, lenient, merciful, clement, indulgent, liberal, humane, kindly, charitable, compassionate, forbearing, sympathetic.

Hazy: *1. Covered by a haze. 2. Vague and unclear.*

Synonym: Indistinct, vague, unclear, blurred, misty, foggy, hidden, obscured, latent, submerged.

Antonym: Clear, distinct, manifest, discernible, perceptible, observable, detectable, noticeable, conspicuous, prominent, obvious.

****

Ideal: *1. Most suitable, perfect. 2. Desirable or perfect in one's imagination.*

Synonym: Perfect, flawless, faultless, fanciful, imaginary, impeccable, matchless, peerless, immaculate.

Antonym: Imperfect, unsuitable, unsound, flawed, defective, blemished, impure, deformed.

Ingenious: *Clever, original and inventive.*

Synonym: Smart, clever, creative, inventive, original, resourceful, shrewd, clever, canny, sharp.

Antonym: Stupid, dull, naïve, ingenuous, unstudied, artless.

Inimical: *Tending to obstruct or harm.*

Synonym: Hostile, harmful, incompatible, antagonistic, aggressive, unfriendly, aloof, cool, cold, ill-disposed, estranged, alienated, opposed, rancorous, bitter, acrimonious, resentful.

Antonym: Friendly, compatible, amicable, warm-hearted, well-meaning, kind, hearty, cordial, congenial, benevolent.

****

J

Jolly: *Happy and cheerful.*

Synonym: Happy, jaunty, joyful, cheerful, merry, cheery.
Antonym: Unhappy, sad, sorrowful, melancholy, depressed, disconsolate, woeful, despondent.

Jovial: *Cheerful and friendly.*

Synonym: Happy, cheerful, cheery, joyous, friendly, high-spirited, chirpy, light-hearted, breezy, carefree, easy-going, radiant, bouncy, sparkling, ebullient, jocular, genial, convivial.
Antonym: Unhappy, dejected, depressed, sad, unfriendly, gloomy, cheerless, morose, glum, miserable, dismal, dispirited, disheartened.

Judicious: *Having or done with sound judgement.*

Synonym: Selective, discerning, fastidious, fussy, careful, mindful, prudent, wary, cautious, circumspect.
Antonym: Injudicious, indiscreet, careless, negligent, neglectful, casual, reckless, imprudent, indiscreet, impetuous.

****

K

Kind: *Considerate and understanding.*

Synonym: Considerate, generous, charitable, benevolent, good, kindly, benign, thoughtful, warm-hearted, compassionate, sympathetic, helpful, obliging, loving, tender, accommodating, affectionate, gracious, courteous.

Antonym: Inconsiderate, harsh, severe, unkind, malevolent, wicked, bad, evil, malignant, baleful, hostile, spiteful, catty, caustic, bitter, acrimonious, vindictive, cruel, savage, brutal, fierce, tough, ruthless, cold, callous, hardhearted, cold-blooded.

Kinship: *1. Blood relationships. 2. A sharing of characteristics or origins.*

Synonym: Relatedness, relevance, pertinence, affinity, affiliation, bond, tie, rapport, connection, relationship, link, tie-up, association, interrelatedness, correlation, inter-dependence.

Antonym: Unrelated, irrelevant, inappropriate, extraneous, foreign, alien, random, unconnected, incidental, tangential, peripheral, inessential, chance, coincidental.

Kudos: *Praise and honour.*

Synonym: Compliments, praise, encomiums, acclaims, esteem, admiration, glory, prestige, honour.

Antonym: Criticism, brickbats, dishonour, discredit, notoriety, infamy, unpopularity, disgrace, shame, dishonour, ignominy.

****

L

Large: *1. Of considerable size. 2. Wide in range or scope.*

Synonym: Huge, mammoth, gargantuan, colossal, quantitative, ample, bulky, big, massive, extensive, capacious, voluminous, sizeable, considerable, king-size, jumbo, outsize, enormous, gigantic, monumental, immense, vast, Brobdingnagian.

Antonym: Small, puny, tiny, insignificant, minute, diminutive, petite, dainty, mini, miniature, pint-sized, wee, Lilliputian, dwarfish, runty, stunted, undersized.

Loud: *1. Making much noise. 2. Strong in expression.*

Synonym: Noisy, vociferous, clamorous, deafening, shrill, uproarious, strident, stentorian, resonant, sonorous, ringing, high-pitched, piercing, ear-splitting, deafening.

Antonym: Soft, low, silent, noiseless, quiet, soundless, hushed, muted, murmured, soft-spoken, indistinct, inaudible, subdued, muffled.

Limitless: *Without boundaries.*

Synonym: Infinite, inexhaustible, boundless, countless, innumerable, incalculable, vast, unfathomable, immeasurable, numberless, untold, endless, indefinite, open-ended, never-ending, interminable, eternal, immortal, perpetual, everlasting.

Antonym: Few, limited, handful, scanty, sparse, infrequent, demarcated, bounded.

****

M

Major: *1. Important, serious, severe. 2. Greater or more important.*

Synonym: Superior, greater, higher, main, best, maximal, optimal, substantial, sizeable, considerable, ample, voluminous, capacious, powerful, mighty.

Antonym: Minor, inferior, lesser, smaller, diminutive, dwarfish, minimal, scant, few, rare, sparse, scarce, paltry, insignificant, trivial, trifling, undersized, puny, feeble, thin, meagre.

Mild: *1. Gentle, not easily provoked. 2. Of moderate level.*

Synonym: Docile, meek, moderate, lenient, calm, gentle, composed, impassive, tame, restrained, soothing, bland, soft, insipid, mellow, tender.

Antonym: Harsh, wild, ferocious, brutish, sharp, rugged, crude, gnarled, coarse, grating.

Morbid: *1. Characterised by an abnormal interest in unhealthy subjects, particularly death and disease. 2. (Medical) Of the nature of or indicative of disease.*

Synonym: Diseased, tainted, poisoned, mangy, rotten, sickly, unhealthy, weakly.

Antonym: Healthy, wholesome, bracing, invigorating, salubrious.

****

N

Nebulous: *1. In the form of a cloud or haze; hazy. 2. Vague or ill-defined.*

Synonym: Obscure, dim, hidden, latent, vague, ambiguous, abstruse, unreal, hazy, shadowy, ghostly, ephemeral, fleeting, tenuous.

Antonym: Clear, lucid, vivid, explicit, real, actual, factual, empirical, historical.

Nervous: *Easily agitated or alarmed.*

Synonym: Hesitant, timid, timorous, agitated, fainthearted, tremulous, anxious, edgy, jittery, jumpy, perturbed, apprehensive, flustered, tremulous, shaky, tense, trembling, fearful, wary, uneasy, worried, concerned, alarmed.

Antonym: Bold, courageous, doughty, fearless, audacious, confident, intrepid, plucky, valiant, heroic, dashing, spunky.

Notorious: *Famous or known for some bad quality or deed.*

Synonym: Infamous, ignominious, disgraceful, disreputable, despicable, shady, shifty, unreliable, untrustworthy, questionable, dubious.

Antonym: Distinguished, noted, honourable, famous, renowned, celebrated, worthy, reputable, meritorious, admirable.

****

Oblivious: *Not aware of what is happening around oneself.*

Synonym: Forgetful, absentminded, inattentive, heedless, careless, unaware, unmindful, unconscious.

Antonym: Attentive, aware, observant, mindful, careful, conscious.

Obstinate: *1. Stubborn refusal to change one's opinion or course of action. 2. Unyielding.*

Synonym: Stubborn, obdurate, inflexible, mulish, unyielding, incorrigible, rigid, recalcitrant.

Antonym: Fickle, indecisive, irresolute, unstable, vacillating.

Odious: *Extremely unpleasant or repulsive.*

Synonym: Hateful, repulsive, horrid, offensive, oppressive, execrable, detestable, obnoxious, loathsome, abominable, repugnant, revolting, disgusting, vile, nasty, abhorrent, abominable.

Antonym: Likeable, attractive, endearing, adorable, winsome, magnetic, delightful, charming, tender, affectionate, lovable.

****

Paltry: *1. Very small or meagre (amount). 2. Petty or trivial.*

Synonym: Tiny, little, diminutive, mean, insignificant, minor, trivial, trifling, puny, feeble, meagre, thin.

Antonym: Great, big, bulky, huge, massive, vast, enormous, immense, mammoth, sizable, considerable, hefty, gigantic, colossal, monumental.

Paramount: *1. Supreme, more important than others. 2. Having supreme power.*

Synonym: Superior, principal, foremost, prominent, leading, chief, main, major, primary.

Antonym: Inferior, minor, subordinate, secondary.

Poor: *1. Lacking sufficient money to live comfortably or as per average standards. 2. Of low or inferior standard or quality.*

Synonym: Impoverished, impecunious, penurious, destitute, penniless, indigent, needy, underprivileged.

Antonym: Rich, affluent, wealthy, prosperous, well-off, well-to-do, moneyed, well-heeled.

Proud: *1. Feeling pride or satisfaction in one's own or another's achievement. 2. Having or showing a high opinion of oneself.*

Synonym: Haughty, condescending, patronising, disdainful, arrogant, overbearing, big-headed, conceited, vainglorious, swollen-headed, snobbish.

Antonym: Humble, meek, self-effacing, modest, unpretentious, unassuming.

****

Query: *A question, especially one that expresses doubt.*

Synonym: Question, enquiry, request, petition, interrogation, investigation, quiz, examination, inquisition, quest, probe, exploration, search, survey, review, scrutiny, inspection, cross-examination, analysis.

Antonym: Answer, reply, reaction, response, acknowledgement, feedback, retort, rejoinder, riposte, back-answer, rebuttal, counter-query, counter-charge, retaliation.

Quick-tempered: *Easily angered.*

Synonym: Hot-headed, impulsive, intolerant, irritable, impatient, high strung.

Antonym: Impassive, imperturbable, phlegmatic, level-headed, unflappable, cool, calm, collected, composed, even-tempered, self-possessed, serene, tranquil, placid, dispassionate, nonchalant.

Quick-witted: *With the ability to think or respond quickly.*

Synonym: Sharp, clever, brilliant, intelligent, bright, brainy, gifted.

Antonym: Dull, mindless, brainless, empty-headed, stupid, slow-witted, moronic.

****

R

Rebellious: *Unmanageable or difficult to control.*

Synonym: Dissenting, quarrelsome, antagonistic, hostile, mutinous, divisive, discordant.

Antonym: Cooperative, helpful, harmonious, concurring, agreeable, peaceful, receptive.

Reckless: *Unconcerned, without thought or care for the consequences of an action.*

Synonym: Negligent, careless, imprudent, indiscreet, impetuous, unscrupulous, unmindful, thoughtless, inconsiderate, inattentive, injudicious.

Antonym: Careful, prudent, discreet, mindful, thoughtful, considerate, attentive, solicitous, cautious, circumspect, judicious, wary, conscientious, thorough, meticulous, scrupulous, methodical, painstaking.

Rowdy: *Noisy and disorderly.*

Synonym: Aggressive, belligerent, boisterous, riotous, indisciplined, unrestrained.

Antonym: Orderly, reasonable, calm, restrained, disciplined, cool, well-behaved.

****

S

Sacred: *1. Holy, connected with a deity and considered worthy of veneration. 2. Religious rather than secular.*

Synonym: Holy, godly, sanctified, hallowed, religious, mystical, spiritual, supernatural.
Antonym: Devilish, unholy, satanic, wicked, Mephisthelean, diabolical, fiendish, infernal, hellish.

Skilful: *Having or exhibiting skill or mastery.*

Synonym: Proficient, expert, accomplished, experienced, conversant, well-versed, efficient.
Antonym: Clumsy, amateurish, inexpert, unskilful, inefficient, bungling, awkward.

Spurious: *1. Something that is false or fake. 2. (An argument or reasoning) Apparently but not actually valid.*

Synonym: Unreal, imaginary, make-believe, fictional, dream-like, hallucinatory, illusory, chimerical, ghostly, delusory, shadowy, specious, phoney, flimsy, hollow, invalid.
Antonym: Real, objective, palpable, tangible, corporeal, solid, concrete, physical, material, actual, natural, factual, historical, true, valid, pure, authentic.

****

T

Tactful: *Having or showing diplomacy or tact.*

Synonym: Civil, decorous, respectable, dignified, polished, courteous, diplomatic, couth, refined, well-mannered, delicate.
Antonym: Tactless, undiplomatic, uncivil, discourteous, rude, crass, boorish, uncouth, caddish, loutish, indecent, indecorous, indelicate, improper.

Temporary: *Lasting for a limited period only.*

Synonym: Fleeting, provisional, transient, transitory, evanescent, makeshift, passing, ephemeral, shortlived, brief, impermanent.
Antonym: Permanent, eternal, perpetual, everlasting, immortal, timeless, deathless, undying, imperishable, indestructible, ageless.

Trite: *(Of an idea or remark) Lacking originality or freshness; dull on account of overexposure or overuse.*

Synonym: Banal, hackneyed, commonplace, platitudinous, repetitive, reiterative, monotonous, routine, stale, trivial, empty, ineffective.

Antonym: Meaningful, significant, telling, emphatic, cogent, incisive, persuasive, effective.

****

Ubiquitous: *Something present, appearing or found everywhere.*

Synonym: Universal, global, commonplace, prevalent, widespread, endemic, omniscient, omnipresent, pervasive.

Antonym: Absent, lacking, devoid, nonexistent, unavailable, empty, vacant, void, missing, deficient.

Unwonted: *Unaccustomed or unusual.*

Synonym: Unaccustomed, unused, unfamiliar, novel, new, strange, unusual, unprecedented, unconventional, unorthodox.

Antonym: Habitual, customary, regular, wonted, usual, familiar, accustomed, commonplace, traditional, conventional, accepted, longstanding, time-honoured.

Upmarket: *Relating to the more affluent or expensive section of the market.*

Synonym: Exclusive, affluent, luxurious, opulent, plush, palatial, pricey.

Antonym: Downmarket, underprivileged, disadvantaged, underdeveloped, cheap, inexpensive.

****

Vacant: *Not occupied, empty.*

Synonym: Absent, empty, void, blank, vacuous, hollow, missing, devoid, deficient, short, unoccupied, deserted, abandoned, depopulated, cleared.

Antonym: Resident, present, occupied, existent, ready, handy, available, attendant.

Valid: *1. Supporting the intended claim. 2. Executed in compliance with the law.*

Synonym: Real, actual, factual, authentic.
Antonym: Invalid, unreal, fake, spurious, unsubstantiated, unproved.

Vociferous: *Vehement or clamorous.*

Synonym: Loud, noisy, clamorous, vehement, strident, resonant, shrill, high-pitched, piercing, deafening, ear-splitting.
Antonym: Faint, soft, low, muted, murmured, indistinct, inaudible, quiet, hushed, muffled, subdued.

****

W

Wane: *To become weaker; decrease or diminish.*

Synonym: Decrease, diminish, slacken, lessen, reduce, deduct, subtract, depreciate, decline, contract, shrink, retrench, deflate, depress, dwindle, ebb, recede, abate, subside, decelerate, fall, dip, drop, plunge, slide, slump, slash, curtail.
Antonym: Wax, increase, grow, add, accrue, accumulate, appreciate, augment, develop, inflate, rise, burgeon, sprout, thrive, prosper, advance, progress, accelerate, spread, enlarge, expand, mushroom, proliferate, multiply, spiral, boost, swell.

Warm-hearted: *Sympathetic and kind.*

Synonym: Friendly, affectionate, amicable, sociable, well-meaning, benevolent, kind, cordial, congenial.
Antonym: Hostile, unfriendly, inimical, antagonistic, aggressive, chilly, cool, cold, alienated, opposed, incompatible, bitter, resentful, acrimonious.

Wily: *Skilled at securing an advantage, especially through cunning and unfair means.*

Synonym: Crafty, cunning, deceitful, dishonest, duplicitous, treacherous, perfidious, tricky, sly, fraudulent, deceptive.
Antonym: Truthful, honest, upright, trustworthy, bona fide, sincere, naïve, artless, guileless, straightforward.

****

Y

Yearn: *Have an intense feeling of loss and longing for something or somebody.*

Synonym: Pine, grieve, mourn, fancy, hanker, thirst, lust, crave (for).
Antonym: Indifference, apathy, aversion, distaste, dislike, unconcern.

Youthful: *Young or seeming young; characteristic of young people.*

Synonym: Young, fresh, ageless, green, callow, coltish.
Antonym: Old, adult, mature, ageing, aged, elderly, geriatric, doddering, senile, white-haired.

Yummy: *Delicious, tasty.*

Synonym: Tasty, savoury, delicious, flavoursome, tempting, appetising, mouth-watering, delectable, palatable.
Antonym: Tasteless, flavourless, insipid, bland, unappetising, unpalatable, inedible, unsavoury, yukky.

****

Z

Zealous: *Having or showing zeal (a fanatical commitment to a religion or cause).*

Synonym: Loyal, faithful, committed, devout, practising, dedicated, earnest, fanatical, fundamentalist, crusading, fervent, enthusiastic.
Antonym: Uncommitted, disloyal, uninterested, unenthusiastic, unfaithful.

Zest: *Great enthusiasm and energy.*

Synonym: Vigour, energy, dynamism, dash, élan, liveliness, enthusiasm, fervour, gusto, relish, initiative, drive, aggressiveness, spirit.
Antonym: Weakness, feebleness, frailty, languor, listlessness, lethargy, lassitude.

Zoom: *Move or travel very quickly.*

Synonym: Hurry, rush, scurry, hustle, scramble, scamper, hasten, expedite, dash, sprint, spurt, race, whiz.
Antonym: Unhurried, slow, dilatory, leisurely, easygoing, phlegmatic, plodding, lazy, sluggish, slothful, languid, tardy.

Mastering Punctuation

Proper punctuation is very important and can make all the difference between communicating your message effectively and creating a communication gap. Punctuation serves the purpose of improving the clarity of a sentence (through the use of a full stop, comma, colon, semi-colon and brackets), indicating words that are not a statement (question mark, exclamation mark, quotation marks), showing how words relate to one another (apostrophe, hyphen) and indicating that a group of letters is an abbreviation (full stop) or that letters are missing (apostrophe).

History records that improper punctuation has even made the difference between life and death.

Full Stop: Also referred to as a *period, point* or *full point*, the primary use of a full stop (.) is to mark the end of a declarative sentence (one that states a fact) or an imperative sentence (one that gives a command or states a request).

Declarative sentence: People stopped visiting theatres after the rates were nearly doubled.

Imperative sentence: Please pass me the salt.

Full stops are also used in some abbreviations: *Sept., i.e., etc.* and *et al.*, amongst others.

If a sentence ends with a question mark or an exclamation mark, one does **not** use a full stop after this, as the question mark or the exclamation mark already contains a full stop within itself.

Comma: The comma (,) is meant to add detail to the structure of sentences and to make their meaning clear by indicating words that either do or do not belong together. The comma usually represents the natural breaks and pauses that a person makes while speaking and it operates at phrase level and word level.

Phrase level: A comma should be used to mark off parts of a sentence that are separated by conjunctions (*and, but, yet,* etc.). The use of a comma is particularly important when there is a change in or a repetition of the subject. An example:
- He was a habitual liar, which is why people never believed what he said.

Word level: A comma is almost always used to separate adjectives having the same range of reference coming before a noun:
- It was a dark, cold, moonless night.
- Adolf Hitler was a ruthless, power-hungry, maniacal person.

Between a pair of adjectives, the comma can be replaced by *and* to impart a stronger effect:
- Adolf Hitler was a ruthless and power-hungry person.

When the adjectives have a different range of reference (e.g., size and colour) or when the last adjective has a closer relation to the noun, the comma is omitted:
- He wore a loose khaki uniform.
- He was a crazy old man.

Commas are used to separate items in a list or sequence:
- The guests were served biscuits, pastries, and tea.

In the above example, a comma has been used before *and*, which some authorities believe is unnecessary and should therefore be avoided. In many cases, however, a comma before *and* helps ensure clarity. Whether to use a comma before *and* or not would therefore depend upon the structure of the sentence.

However, the comma must be left out between nouns that occur together in the same grammatical role in a sentence (termed *apposition*):
- His son Ajay went on to become a pilot.

But a comma needs to be used when the noun is an additional piece of information that could be deleted from a sentence without affecting the meaning:

- His father, Rajinder Bhimsain Sawhney, was a Station Master.

Semicolon: This is possibly one of the trickiest signs to use for writers, which is why you will find its usage the least. However, if properly used, the semicolon can be one of the most useful and significant punctuation marks.

The semicolon (;) is basically a punctuation mark that indicates a more pronounced pause than that indicated by a comma but less important than that of a full stop. In essence, a semicolon divides two parts of a sentence that balance each other, and could stand independently too.

For instance, consider this sentence:

- He seemed in a foul mood. So, I fled the scene.

The above two sentences make perfect sense by themselves. However, we could use a semicolon to join these conveniently:

- He seemed in a foul mood; so, I fled the scene.

The semicolon can also be used to replace a comma in a sentence in order to indicate a stronger division. However, semicolons cannot be used if two thoughts are not connected in some way or the other. Semicolons also cannot be employed if one of the sentences is not a complete one in itself.

Colon: Unlike its cousin, the semicolon, the colon (:) is used more often in formal print, but not as frequently in daily writing. The colon is a punctuation mark that's used to precede a list of items, a quotation, or an expansion or explanation. While a semicolon links two balanced statements, a colon flows conveniently from the first statement to the second. Usually, it links a general or introductory statement to an example, or a cause to an effect or a premise with a conclusion.

For example, consider the following sentence:

- The tour operator said his package included: to and fro air tickets, a complimentary drink on arrival, breakfast, evening snacks and dinner, hotel accommodation.

A colon is sometimes used to indicate more emphasis in direct speech:

- The madman screamed: "I am not mad! The voice of God commanded me to slay."

Besides, in American English, a colon is used in the initial greeting of a letter:

- Dear Mr Randhawa:

However, in British or Indian English, a comma is used:

- Dear Mr Randhawa,

But by far, the most common use of a colon is to indicate to the reader that a list of items now follows:

- The schoolchildren were told to bring the following items for the picnic: a torch, a sleeping bag, two sets of night clothes, three panties/underwear, water bottle, three hankies and a lunchbox.

There are other uses of a colon too. It is used to divide the title of a book from the subtitle; between the hours and minutes when writing the time; in differentiating the chapter and verse in the Bible or the *Bhagavad Gita* and other similar instances.

Question Mark:
A question mark (?) is mainly used to indicate a direct question:

- Are you reading this book?

It can also be used in a sentence that ends with a question:

- You are involved in the crime too, aren't you?

The question mark is sometimes also used when a question is worded like a statement:

- I wonder if it's worth calling him?

In instances where there is doubt or uncertainty about a name, date or word, the question mark is used to indicate this:

- Mullah Nasruddin (?1208-1284) was one of the world's most loved tricksters.

The question mark preceding the year of birth indicates that Mullah Nasruddin's year of birth is uncertain.

And although it may seem like an error, a series of questions that are not complete sentences should have a question mark after each fragment:

Can you believe that he is an inveterate liar? or that he is not working? or that he had never taken up a job in the first place? or that he never ever has any money?

However, question marks should not be used in some situations where it may seem that the use is required. The exceptions include indirect questions, where the question is reported rather than directly expressed:
- He inquired what time it was.

Rhetorical questions (a question asked for effect or to make a statement rather than to elicit information) also may not require a question mark:
- Why ducks sleep on one leg.
- How the tiger got its stripes.

Rhetorical questions don't require a question mark since they are simply meant for effect and don't call for an answer.

Exclamation Mark: The exclamation mark (!) is simply a punctuation mark that indicates an exclamation. The statement could also be one expressing shock or surprise. In essence, the mark indicates in writing what one would verbally say by shouting or speaking strongly, either to attract attention or to emphasise a point.

There are quite a few ways to use this mark. For instance, a parent warning the child and trying to enforce discipline might say:
- Behave yourself!

Or you could indicate the expression of a strong feeling of surprise, absurdity, approval, disapproval, regret and a host of other emotions:
- What a horrible thing to do!
- How crazy of him to have done such a thing!
- Where the hell is he?!

In the above examples, words like *how* or *what* precede the sentence. The last sentence is preceded by *where*, and ends with a question mark as well as an exclamation mark, which is one of the rare usages. Such a sentence denotes both the element of questioning and of surprise.

You could also use the exclamation mark to express a wish or a feeling of regret:
- ❏ The kids would have loved to tag along!
- ❏ If only you had informed me in advance!

A note of caution, though... In day-to-day writing, the exclamation mark is used sparingly. Using it too often detracts from proper usage. Besides, it will be counterproductive to attempt adding a false sense of drama or excitement to a style of writing that is routine, unexciting or prosaic.

Quotation Marks: The quotation mark (" ") is also called an *inverted comma*. It consists of the double quotation mark (shown in the preceding sentence) and the single quotation mark (' '). Quotation marks are used either to mark the beginning and end of quotation or title, or to indicate slang usage or words that are jargon.

The most common use is to tell the reader the exact words spoken by a person, which is called a *direct quotation*. For instance:
- ❏ He told me, "I will come to work an hour late today."

The above sentence is a direct quote. As an *indirect quote* it would be stated in this way:
- ❏ He told me that he would come to work an hour late today.

In the above example, the quotation marks are not used since it is an indirect statement. Although both sentences convey exactly the same meaning, in the first instance they tell the reader that the person quoted has spoken directly.

In common writing, only the double quotation mark is used. However, in the print media, the double and single quotation marks are both used, depending on the context. The usage in Britain and America differs, but we shall restrict ourselves to the usage in India, where double quotes are almost always used to indicate direct speech. Single quotes are usually used to indicate a quote within a quote or to indicate that the person quoted has expressed a sentiment mentally rather than verbally. For instance:

- "Shweta told me, 'Why should I help you out,'" Ramesh informed Harish.

In the above sentence, Ramesh speaks directly to Harish and tells him what Shweta told him. Therefore, Ramesh's words are used in double quotation marks, while Shweta's directly quoted words are used in single quotation marks. The simple rule of thumb is that if the direct quotes are in double quotation marks, any quote within this quote will then be in single quotation marks. The rule would also apply vice versa, i.e., a direct quote in single quotation marks that includes another quote within would then have the inclusive quote in double quotation marks.

A common error made with quotation marks is that users tend to put the punctuation marks *after* closing the quotes:

- He was furious and told me, "Get lost"!

The above punctuation usage is incorrect. The correct usage would be with the exclamation mark coming before the quotes are closed:

- He was furious and told me, "Get lost!"

The only time one could use the punctuation mark after the quotes close is when the quote is incomplete:

- Gita was furious and swore that she would get even with me "at all costs".

In this example, Gita's words have not been quoted directly or completely. Just a few of her words have been quoted word for word and are indicated in double quotes. In such instances, closing the double quote after the punctuation mark would be incorrect. The above rules reflect Indian usage.

When quoted words are broken up or interrupted by a reporting verb such as *say*, *said*, *told*, *informed*, etc., the quotation marks would be given in this manner:

- "What I would love to have," Ramit told Sheela, "is a steaming hot cup of coffee."

In this instance, note the usage of the commas before closing the first double quote and after *Sheela*, since both sentences connect the same thought. However, if they were two independent thoughts, the sentence would be written in this manner:

- ❏ "There is something that I would love to have," Ramit told Sheela. "And that is a steaming hot cup of coffee."

The beauty of the above example though, lies in the fact that it could be used following the rules of the previous example and would still not read amiss, purely because the conjunctive word *And* has been used:

- ❏ "There is something that I would love to have," Ramit told Sheela, "and that is a steaming hot cup of coffee."

Another rule to remember with quotes (which is a common error even media pundits and editors make) is that when a person is speaking and it runs into several paragraphs, successive paragraphs will all have the opening quotation mark, but *the closing quotation mark will only be used in the last paragraph*. Closing the quotation mark after each paragraph when the same person is speaking is incorrect and creates confusion in the reader's mind whether the same person is speaking or different persons have been quoted.

Single or double quotation marks are also used to indicate the title of a movie, book, article, poem, serial, etc. In such instances, there is no fixed rule and depending on personal preference or an in-house style, single or double quotation marks may be used.

However, there are many who prefer not to use quotation marks to indicate titles and instead use *italics* for this purpose.

Single or double quotation marks are also used when indicating slang terms and jargon or words from Hindi or any other language other than English.

Apostrophe: The apostrophe (') is a punctuation mark that is used to indicate either possession (e.g., Rajeev's diary) or the omission of letters or numbers (e.g., can't; August '04).

Singular nouns indicate the possessive by adding 's: the tiger's roar (indicating one tiger). Plural nouns indicate the possessive by adding an apostrophe after the *s*: tigers' roars (indicating more than one tiger).

If the plural noun ends in an alphabet other than *s*, the possessive is indicated by adding *'s*: the lion's roar, the kitten's meowing etc.

While apostrophes have a specific use, many misuse them more often. For instance, ordinary plural words don't need an apostrophe, but many end up using them here:

- Price's, worry's, movie's etc.

The correct usage with these plural forms would read:

- Prices, worries, movies etc.

Apostrophes are also used in contractions (*can't* for *cannot*), which is where people also tend to get confused. The most common confusion is with the possessive *whose* with *who's*. *Who's* is simply a contraction of *who is*.

- Who's fault is it?

The above sentence is incorrect. The correct usage is:

- Whose fault is it?

Another problem that users face is with names that end with an *s*: *Thomas, Charles, Vikas, Ulhas,* etc. The confusion here has much to do with the awkward sound that results. In such cases, you could either write the names: *Thomas'* and *Ulhas'* or *Thomas's* and *Ulhas's*. However, it is preferable to use the second option in such cases.

Apostrophes should not be used in the pronouns *hers, its, ours, yours* and *theirs*. This would be an incorrect way to end a letter:

- Your's truly.

The correct way would be:

- Yours truly.

Likewise, watch out for: *its* and *it's*. *Its* (without an apostrophe) is a possessive that denotes *belonging to it*. *It's* (with an apostrophe) is a contraction of *it is*.

- The dog is expecting *it's* dinner.
- The dog is expecting *its* dinner.

In the above examples, the first sentence is incorrect.

Other examples of contractions with an apostrophe are:

Full Form	Contraction
Is not	Isn't
Cannot	Can't
He will	He'll
You have	You've
He is	He's
They are	They're
You all	You'll
Were not	Weren't

In all the above examples, you would need to be careful to ensure you don't misuse the words.

Hyphens: A hyphen is a sign (-) that's used to join words to indicate that they have a combined meaning or that they are grammatically linked, or to indicate a word that has been split up at the end of a line. In print, a hyphen is half the length of a dash. In actual writing, though, there is little noticeable difference between a dash and a hyphen. The purpose of both signs is exactly the opposite, however.

The dash is used to separate words or a group of words, while the hyphen is used to link words or parts of words.

The hyphen is used to join two or more words in order to form a single word (called a compound word): *good-for-nothing, free-for-all, sweet-and-sour, multi-purpose*, etc. Or to join words that have a grammatical relationship which form a compound: *point-blank, load bearing*, etc.

However, even at the end of sentences, always avoid hyphenating acronyms, numbers, contractions and Internet or email addresses.

Dashes: A dash (— or -) allows a writer to introduce informality in writing or to add emphasis, by allowing a sudden change in thought or tone. For instance:

- Let us go to the market and do some shopping. I've run out of hankies and could do with a set of new—oops! I just recalled—today is Monday and the markets this side of town are closed.

The dash indicates to readers that the speaker's train of thought has been suddenly interrupted by something important that he's just recalled.

In published writing, there are two kinds of dash: the *shorter en-dash* (-) or the *longer em-dash* (—). Most word-processing programmes can distinguish between the two lengths of dashes, but in day-to-day writing no such distinction is made. Even many DTP (desktop publishing) and editorial persons do not know the difference.

In printing, the en-dash has certain specific uses (e.g., to indicate a range of numbers or dates, as in 1935-55), whereas the em-dash is the one that is generally used to serve the purpose of a regulation dash.

A pair of dashes is used to indicate asides and parentheses, which indicates a more distinct break than would be possible with commas:

- He was an excellent writer—although he had never gone to school—and had learnt the three R's at home.

As a general rule, when the em-dash is used (as in the above example) there is no space between the dash and the words. However, if an en-dash is used, a single character space is left on either side. For instance, the same sentence would appear this way with an en-dash:

- He was an excellent writer - although he had never gone to school - and had learnt the three R's at home.

Although in many cases a colon could be used to punctuate a sentence and achieve the same effect as a dash, in general it is better to reserve the colon for formal writing.

Brackets or Parentheses: The brackets that are almost always used in writing are the round brackets or parentheses ().

Round brackets are used when the writer wants to indicate explanations and additional information or comments:

- Harish was upset with Deepak and felt like giving him a piece of his mind (to cut him down to size) in the presence of the others. However, he refrained from doing so (he did not wish to precipitate matters).

Or they are used to show optional words that imply doubt or caution:

- There were many (hidden) dangers on the road ahead, and he knew this for sure.

The round brackets are also used to give references or statistical information:

- The Second World War (1939-1945) was the bloodiest conflict in human history.

Square brackets [] are used very infrequently. The usage is restricted to occasions when some additional information has been provided, often by someone other than the writer (usually an editor) of the original text, to clarify an obscure point or to add extra information that facilitates better understanding or ease of reading.

- Anil Ambani claims that the Ambani brothers are not inheritors [of Dhirubhai Ambani's legacy] but partners.

These are the most common punctuation signs that new English readers would encounter on the highway to mastering English. Once you master the usage of these punctuation marks, the written words would flow faster and more easily.

∞

Homonyms

Words that sound like one another can be fun, particularly when they are pronounced the same way but spelt differently. Such words are categorised as *Homonyms*.

The Concise Oxford Dictionary defines a *homonym* as: *each of two or more words having the same spelling or pronunciation but different meanings and origins* (e.g. *Pole* and *Pole*). One Pole refers to a citizen of Poland, who could either be referred to as *Polish* or a *Pole*. The second Pole refers to a bamboo *pole* or any other wooden *pole*.

Homonyms are good friends of writers specialising in humour, since they make excellent raw material for puns.

Let's take an alphabetical walk down the Homonym Lane and discover the different homonyms that ambush us along the way.

- **Ad:** A short form of the word *advertisement*.
  Add: A short form of the word *addition*.
- **Aid:** To help or assist somebody.
  Aide: An assistant (usually to a political leader).
- **Aero:** Of an aircraft, the preceding word of the word *aeroplane*, used in British-Indian English, unlike the American *airplane*.
  Arrow: A slender, pointed shaft, as in *bow and arrow*.
- **Ail:** To be ill or sick.
  Ale: A beer.

- **Aisle:** A walkway.
  Isle: An island.
- **Allowed:** That which is permitted.
  Aloud: Spoken in a loud manner.
- **Altar:** A raised platform used as a place of worship.
  Alter: To change.
- **Arc:** A portion of a circle.
  Ark: A water-borne vessel (for instance, Noah's Ark, referred to in the Bible).
- **Ascent:** A climb.
  Assent: To agree or give permission to.
- **Ate:** Past tense of the word *eat*.
  Eight: The number that comes after seven and before nine.
- **Awed:** In a state of wonder.
  Odd: Not the usual, not the norm.
- **Aye:** A response accepting an order (naval term).
  Eye: An organ of sight.
  I: Oneself, first person singular, used by a person to refer to himself or herself.

****

B

- **Bail: 1.** The temporary release of an accused person awaiting trial, sometimes on the condition that a sum of money is deposited in the court to guarantee their appearance in court at a future date. **2.** To scoop water out of a ship or boat. **3.** To make an emergency descent by parachute from an aircraft. **4.** To rescue someone or something from difficulty.
  Bale: A bundle of hay or dry grass.
- **Bait: 1.** Food used to entice fish or other animals as prey. **2.** To deliberately annoy, taunt or torment somebody.
  Bate: (Of a hawk) Beat wings in agitation and flutter off a perch (term used in falconry).

- **Bald:** A hairless person.
  Bawled: To have cried loudly.
- **Band 1.** A small group of musicians and vocalists. **2.** A group of people who have a common interest or purpose.
  Banned: Something that is disallowed or illegal.
- **Bard:** A poet, traditionally one reciting epics (*the Bard* is a reference to William Shakespeare).
  Barred: 1. Enclosed by poles or bars. **2.** Prohibit from doing something or going somewhere.
- **Bare:** Naked or without any covering.
  Bear: 1. A large heavy mammal of the family *Ursidae*, of which there are several species, the largest being the Kodiak Bear of the Arctic regions. **2.** (Stock Exchange) A person who sells shares hoping to buy them back later at a lower price.
  Bear: 1. Manage to tolerate (pain or problem etc.) **2.** Give birth to (a child).
- **Bark:** The tough outer covering of a tree.
- **Bark: 1.** The sharp explosive cry of a dog, fox or seal. **2.** To utter (a command or order) abruptly and aggressively.
- **Barque:** A sailing ship, typically with three masts.
- **Baron: 1.** A member of the lowest order of British nobility, minor royalty. **2.** A powerful person in business or industry (for instance, a *press baron* or a *liquor baron*).
  Barren: 1. (Of land) Too poor or infertile to produce much or any vegetation. **2.** (Of a tree or plant) Not producing any fruit or seed. **3.** (Of a female animal or woman) Unable to bear offspring or a child. **4.** Bleak and lifeless.
- **Baul:** Singing minstrels of Bengal and Bangladesh.
  Bawl: 1. To shout noisily or angrily. **2.** To weep noisily.
- **Beach: 1.** A pebbly or sandy shore at the edge of the sea or a lake. **2.** To bring onto the beach from water.
  Beech: A large tree with smooth grey bark, glossy leaves and hard, pale, fine-grained wood.

- **Berry:** A small juicy fruit without a stone.
  Bury: 1. Put or hide underground. **2.** Place a dead body in the earth or a tomb. **3.** Cause to disappear or to become unnoticeable. **4.** Involve oneself deeply in something.
- **Berth: 1.** A ship's allotted place at a wharf or dock. **2.** Moor or moored in a *berth*. **3.** Provide a berth for (a passenger on a train).
  Birth: 1. The emergence of a baby or other young creature from the body of its mother; the start of life as a physically separate being. **2.** The beginning of something; origin, descent or ancestry.
- **Better:** Superior; in a more advanced state.
  Bettor: A person who plays or places a bet.
- **Bite: 1.** Use the teeth to cut into something. **2.** (Of a fish) Take the bait on the end of a fishing line into the mouth. **3.** (Of a policy or situation) Take effect, with unpleasant consequences.
  Byte: (Computing) A group of binary digits or bits (usually eight) operated on as a unit.
- **Bloc:** An alliance or group (of political parties or countries).
  Block: 1. A large solid piece of hard material with flat surfaces on each side. **2.** A large single building subdivided into separate flats or offices. **3.** An obstacle to the smooth or normal progress or functioning of something.
- **Boar:** A wild pig found in the jungle.
  Boer: A South African of Dutch descent.
  Boor: A rough and bad-mannered person; a tasteless buffoon.
  Bore: 1. To make a hole in something. **2.** The hollow part inside a gun barrel or other tube **3.** A dull and uninteresting person or activity. **4.** Make somebody feel weary and uninterested by virtue of being dull and tedious.
- **Board: 1.** A long, thin, flat piece of wood used for floors or other building purposes. **2.** The decision-making body of an organisation. **3.** The provision of regular meals in return for payment or services. **4.** Get on or into (a train, aircraft, ship etc.).
  Bored: Weary of or uninterested in (somebody or something).
- **Bolder:** More courageous or braver (than somebody else).
  Boulder: A large rock.

- **Bole:** A tree trunk.
  Bowl: A dish.
- **Boos:** Disparaging sounds or calls from fans.
  Booze: Alcohol or liquor.
- **Borough:** A town.
  Burrow: 1. A hole or tunnel dug by a small animal as a dwelling. **2.** To dig into or through something solid.
- **Bough:** A main branch of a tree.
  Bow: 1. A knot tied with two loops and two loose ends. **2.** A weapon for shooting arrows that is made of a curved piece of wood joined at both ends by a taut string.
  Bow: 1. Lower the head or bend the upper part of the body as a sign of respect, greeting or shame. **2.** Cause to bend with age or under a heavy weight. **3.** Give in to pressure or demands **4.** Withdraw or retire from something (to *bow out*).
- **Bouy:** A navigational aid.
  Boy: A male child.
- **Breach: 1.** An act of breaking a law, agreement, or code of conduct. **2.** A gap in a wall or barrier, especially one made by an attacking army.

  Breech: 1. The part of a cannon behind the bore. **2.** The back part of a rifle or gun barrel.
- **Bread: 1.** Food make of flour, water and yeast, mixed together and baked. **2.** (Informal) Money.
  Bred: Manner of upbringing – the past tense of *breed*.
- **Broach:** To raise (a sensitive) a subject for discussion.
  Brooch: An ornament fastened to clothing with a hinged pin and catch.

****

C

- **Cache:** A hidden store of things.
  Cash: Money in coins or notes.

- **Cannon: 1.** A large heavy piece of artillery formerly used in warfare. **2.** (Billiards or snooker) A stroke in which the cue ball strikes two balls successively. **3.** Collide with something forcefully or at an angle.

  Canon: 1. A general rule or principle by which something is judged; a Church decree or law. **2.** A collection or list of sacred books accepted as genuine.

- **Canvas:** A strong, coarse unbleached cloth used to make sails, tents, etc. and as a surface for oil painting.

  Canvass: 1. Solicit votes from (electors). **2.** Propose (an idea or plan) for discussion.

- **Capital: 1.** The most important city or town of a country or region, usually the seat of government and administration; a place particularly associated with a specified activity. **2.** Wealth owned by a person or an organisation or invested, lent or borrowed. **3.** A capital letter. **4.** (Of an offence or charge) Liable to attract the death penalty (e.g., He was sentenced to *capital punishment* – death).

  Capitol: 1. (In the US) A building housing a legislative assembly. **2.** (The Capitol) The temple of Jupiter on the Capitoline Hill in ancient Rome.

- **Carat: 1.** A unit of weight for precious stones and pearls, equivalent to 200 milligrams. **2.** (US spelling also *karat*) A measure of the purity of gold, pure gold being 24 carats.

  Caret: A proofreader's mark (^) placed below a line of text to indicate a proposed insertion or correction.

  Carrot: A tapering orange-coloured root eaten as a vegetable.

- **Cast: 1.** Throw forcefully in a specified direction. **2.** Cause (light or shadow) to appear on a surface **3.** Discard. **4.** Shape (metal or other material) by pouring into a mould while molten. **5.** Register (a vote). **6.** Throw the hooked and baited end of a fishing line into the water. **7.** Cast a magic spell to take effect. **8.** The actors taking part in a play or film.

  Caste: 1. Each of the hereditary classes of Hindu society, distinguished by relative degrees of ritual purity or pollution (untouchability) and of social status. **2.** (In some social insects)

A physically distinct kind of individual with a particular function (entomology).

- **Cede:** Give up (power or territory).
  Seed: A plant's unit of reproduction through which another plant is capable of growing.

- **Cell: 1.** A small room in which a prisoner is kept locked or in which a monk or nun sleeps. **2.** A small group of people forming a nucleus of political activity. **3.** A device containing electrodes immersed in electrolyte, used for current generation or electrolysis.
  Sell: Give or hand over in exchange for money.

- **Censor:** An official who examines material that is to be published or a film to be screened and deletes or edits parts considered offensive to societal sensitivities or a threat to security.
  Sensor: A device which detects or measures a physical property.

- **Cite: 1.** Quote (a book or author) as evidence for an argument or belief. **2.** Praise for a courageous act in an official dispatch.
  Sight: 1. The faculty or power of seeing. **2.** The action or fact of seeing someone or something.
  Site: 1. An area of ground on which something is located. **2.** A place where a particular event or activity is occurring or has occurred.

- **Coarse: 1.** Rough or harsh in texture, unrefined. **2.** (Of a person's features) Not elegantly formed or well proportioned. **3.** (Of a person or their speech) Rude or vulgar.
  Course: 1. The route or direction followed by a ship, aircraft, road or river. **2.** The way in which something progresses or develops. **3.** A dish forming one of the successive parts of a meal. **4.** A series or lectures or lessons in a particular subject. **5.** An area of land prepared for racing, golf or any other sport.

- **Complacent:** Smug and uncritically satisfied with oneself or one's achievements, self-satisfied.
  Complaisant: Willingness to please others or to accept their behaviour without protest.

- **Complement: 1.** A thing that contributes extra features to something else and thereby enhances and improves it. **2.** The number or quantity that makes something complete.

Compliment: A polite expression of praise or admiration.

- **Conch:** A tropical marine mollusc.
  Conk: 1. (Of a machine) Break down (*conk out* - informal). **2.** Faint or go to sleep; die.
- **Coo: 1.** (Of a pigeon or dove) Make a soft murmuring sound. **2.** (Of a person) To speak in a soft gentle voice.
  Coup: 1. A sudden and violent seizure of power from a government. **2.** An unexpected and notably successful act.

****

D

- **Dammed:** Hold back or obstruct, to prevent water from flowing.
  Damned: (Informal) Used to emphasise one's anger or frustration, cursed.
- **Days:** Two or more days.
  Daze: Make unable to think or react properly, a state of stunned confusion.
- **Dew:** Tiny drops of water that form on cool surfaces at night, when atmospheric vapour condenses.
  Due: 1. Expected at, planned for, or required by a certain time. **2.** Proper, appropriate. **3.** (*Dues*) Fees.
- **Discreet: 1.** Careful or prudent in speech or actions, especially in order to avoid giving offence or attracting attention. **2.** Unobtrusive.
  Discrete: Individually separate and distinct.
- **Doe: 1.** A female deer. **2.** A female hare, rabbit, rat, ferret or kangaroo.
  Dough: 1. A thick malleable mixture of flour and liquid (water or milk) for baking into bread or pastry. **2.** (Informal) Money.
- **Doc:** Short form of *doctor*, a physician.
  Dock: 1. An enclosed area of water in a port for the loading, unloading and repair of ships. **2.** To come or bring (a ship) into a dock. **3.** The enclosure in a criminal court where the defendant stands or sits. **4.** Deduct (money or point in a score) **5.** Cut short (an animal's tail).

- **Draft: 1.** A preliminary version of a piece of writing, a plan or sketch. **2.** A written order to pay a specified amount. **3.** (The draft) Compulsory recruitment for military service (US).
  Draught: 1. A current of cool air in a room or confined place. **2.** A single act of drinking or inhaling. **3.** Denoting beer served from a cask rather than from a bottle or can. **4.** Denoting an animal used for pulling heavy loads.
- **Dual:** Consisting of two parts, elements or aspects.
  Duel: 1. (Historical) A pre-arranged contest with deadly weapons between two persons to settle a point of honour. **2.** (Modern) A contest between two parties.

****

E

- **Ewe:** A female sheep.
  Yew: A coniferous tree.
- **Eyelet:** A small round hole in leather or cloth for threading a lace, string or rope through.
  Islet: A small island.

****

F

- **Faint:** To pass out or become unconscious.
  Feint: A deceptive or pretended blow, thrust or attacking movement, especially in boxing or fencing.
- **Fair: 1.** Treating people equally, just or appropriate in the circumstances. **2.** (Of hair or complexion) Light. **3.** Considerable in size or amount, moderately good. **4.** (Of weather) Fine and dry **5.** A gathering of stalls and amusements for public entertainment. **6.** A periodic gathering for the sale of goods.
  Fare: 1. The money a passenger on public transport has to pay. **2.** A range of fare. **3.** To perform in a specified way in a particular situation or period.
- **Farrow:** A litter of pigs; (of a sow) to give birth to (piglets).
  Pharaoh: Egyptian kings of ancient times.

- **Faze:** (Usually with the negative) Disturb or disconcert (informal).
  Phase: A part of the sequence, a particular period.
- **Feat:** An achievement or accomplishment.
  Feet: The plural form of *foot* – the lower extremity of the leg below the ankle.
- **Feted:** Honoured or entertained lavishly.
  Fetid: Smelling unpleasant.
- **Few:** Not many, less in number.
  Phew: An expression of relief, usually with an exclamation mark.
- **Flair: 1.** Natural ability or talent. **2.** Stylishness.
  Flare: 1. A sudden brief burst of flame or light. **2.** A device producing a very bright flame as a signal or marker. **3.** A sudden burst of intense emotion or anger. **4.** A gradual widening towards the hem of a garment.
- **Flea:** A small wingless jumping insect, which feeds on the blood of mammals and birds.
  Flee: To run away.
- **Flour:** A powder obtained by grinding grain, used to make bread, cakes and pastries.
  Flower: A bloom of a plant.
- **Foreword:** The introduction to a book.
  Forward: To move ahead.
- **Foul: 1.** Offensive to the senses. **2.** Contrary to the rules of a sport. **3.** Polluted or contaminated. .
  Fowl: A domesticated bird derived from a junglefowl and kept for its egg or meat, a cock or hen.

****

G

- **Gait:** A person's manner of walking.
  Gate: A hinged barrier used to close an opening in a wall, fence or hedge.

- **Gild:** To cover or coat thinly with guild.
  Gilled: Having *gills* – the paired respiratory organ of fish and some amphibians through which oxygen is extracted from water.
  Guild: An association of people in pursuit of a common guild or mutual aid.
- **Gin:** An alcoholic beverage.
  Jinn: (In Arabian and Islamic mythology) An intelligent spirit that can appear in human and animal form (also spelt *djinn*).
- **Grill: 1.** A device on a cooker that radiates heat downwards for cooking food. **2.** A gridiron used for cooking food on an open fire. **3.** A dish of food, particularly meat, cooked using a grill. **4.** (Informal) Subject someone to intense questioning or interrogation.

****

H

- **Hail: 1.** Pellets of frozen rain falling in showers. **2.** A large number of things that are hurled forcefully through the air. **3.** Call out to someone to attract attention. **4.** Acclaim enthusiastically as something. **5.** Have one's origins or home in (*to hail from*).
  Hale: (Usually referring to an old person) Strong and healthy (*hale and hearty*).
- **Hall:** A large room.
  Haul: 1. To pull or drag with effort or force. **2.** A quantity of something obtained, especially illegally. **3.** A number of fish caught at one time (*a good haul*). **4.** A distance to be travelled (*it is a long haul*).
- **Hangar:** A garage for aircraft.
  Hanger: A shaped piece of wood, plastic or metal with a hook at the top, meant for hanging clothes.
- **Heal:** To cure a disease.
  Heel: The hind part of the foot.
- **Heard: 1.** Sound picked up by the ear. **2.** To be told or informed about.

Herd: Large group of animals, especially hoofed mammals, that live together or are kept together.

- **Hoard: 1.** A store of money or valued objects. **2.** To amass and hide or store away (wealth or money).

  Horde: 1. (Mainly derogatory) A large group of people. **2.** An army or tribe of nomadic warriors.

- **Hoes:** More than one long-handled gardening tool with a thin metal blade, used mainly for weeding.

  Hose: 1. A flexible tube conveying water, used primarily for watering plants and in firefighting. **2.** To water or spray with a hose.

- **Holy:** Something considered pure and sacred with religious significance.

  Wholly: Completely, fully or entirely.

- **Humerus:** The bone of the upper arm or forelimb, between the shoulder and the elbow – also called the *funny bone*.

  Humorous: Causing amusement, funny, having or showing a sense of humour.

****

I

- **Idle: 1.** Avoiding work; lazy; (of money) held in cash or in an account paying no interest. **2.** Having no purpose or basis (*idle boast/threat*).

  Idol: 1. An image or representation of a god used as an object of worship. **2.** Something that is adulated (*a sports idol*).

  Idyll: 1. A period or situation that is blissful. **2.** A picturesque scene or incident described in short in verse or prose.

- **In: 1.** Something that is enclosed or surrounded. **2.** Referring to a period of time during which an incident took place. **3.** Expressing the condition of inclusion or involvement.

  Inn: A hotel or public house, traditionally also providing food and lodging.

- **Inc.:** The short form or abbreviation for *incorporated*.

  Ink: A coloured fluid that is used for writing, drawing or printing.

- **Incite:** To encourage or stir up (behaviour that is violent and unlawful).

  Insight: 1. The ability or capacity to gain an accurate, deep and intuitive understanding of something. **2.** An understanding of the above kind.

****

J

- **Jean: 1.** A heavy twilled cotton cloth, especially denim. **2.** A pair of jeans.

  Gene: (Biology) A hereditary unit that is transferred from parent to offspring and which determines the characteristics of the offspring, particularly a distinct sequence of DNA forming part of a chromosome.

- **Jack:** An English or Christian name.

  Jack: 1. A device used for lifting heavy objects, especially one for raising the axle of a motor vehicle. **2.** Playing card bearing an image of soldier, page or knave and normally ranking below the queen.

****

K

- **Knead: 1.** To work dough or clay with the hands. **2.** Massage as if kneading.

  Need: Something one must have, something required.

- **Knight: 1.** (Middle Ages) A man elevated to honourable military rank after service as a page or squire. **2.** A man devoted to the cause or service of a woman (poetic or literary). **3.** A chess piece, shaped like a horse's head, that moves by jumping to the opposite corner of a rectangle two squares by three.

  Night: 1. The time from sunset to sunrise. **2.** The darkness of the night.

- **Knot: 1.** A fastening that is made by looping a piece of string, rope, etc. on itself and tightening it. **2.** A hard lump of bodily tissue. **3.** A small group of people. **4.** A unit of speed equal to one nautical mile per hour, used for ships, aircraft or wind.

Nought: 1. The digit zero. **2.** Nothing.
Not: A word denoting negation.

****

L

- **Lacks:** A thing that does not have or is devoid of (something).
  Lax: 1. Relaxed (of muscles). **2.** Not sufficiently strict, severe (in discipline) or careful.

- **Lessen:** To reduce or bring down in number.
  Lesson: A thing that is learnt; a period of learning or teaching.

- **Liar:** A person who tells lies or falsehoods.
  Lyre: A stringed instrument, used especially in ancient Greece.

- **Lichen: 1.** A fungus that grows on rocks, walls and trees. **2.** A skin disease in which small, round, hard lesions occur close together.
  Liken: To compare (to something).

- **Lightening:** To reduce the weight of (something).
  Lightning: A brief, natural, high-voltage electrical discharge between a cloud and the ground or within a cloud accompanied by a bright flash and often with thunder also.

- **Load: 1.** Heavy or bulky thing that is being carried. **2.** A weight or source of pressure. **3.** The amount of work to be done by a person or machine.
  Lode: A vein of metal ore in the earth.

- **Loan: 1.** A thing that is borrowed, particularly a sum of money that is to be paid back with interest. **2.** The act of lending.
  Lone: By itself, the only one.

****

M

- **Main:** Chief in size or importance.
  Mane: The growth of long hair on the neck of a horse, lion or other animal; a person's long hair.

- **Maize:** A cereal plant that yields corn.

Maze: 1. A network of paths and hedges designed as a puzzle through which a person has to find his way. **2.** A confusing mass of information.

- **Mall: 1.** A large enclosed shopping area where traffic is not permitted. **2.** A sheltered walk or promenade.

  Maul: 1. (Of an animal) To wound by scratching and tearing. **2.** Handle or treat savagely and roughly.

  Moll: 1. A gangster's female companion. **2.** A prostitute or commercial sex worker.

- **Manner: 1.** A specific way in which something is done or happens. **2.** A style in literature or art. **3.** A person's outward bearing or way of behaving with others.

  Manor: 1. A large country house with lands. **2.** (Historical) A unit of land, usually a feudal lordship, consisting of a lord's demesne and lands rented to tenants. **3.** (Informal) One's home territory or area of operation.

- **Medal:** A medal disc with an inscription or design, awarded to acknowledge distinctive achievement or made to commemorate an event.

  Meddle: To interfere in something that does not concern one (usually *meddle in/with*).

- **Might: 1.** Expressing the possibility of (something). **2.** Great power or strength.

  Mite: 1. A tiny arachnid with four pairs of legs. **2.** A small child or animal. **3.** A very small amount.

- **Miner:** A person who works in a mine.

  Minor: With little importance, seriousness or significance.

****

N

- **Naval:** Of, in or relating to a navy or navies.

  Navel: 1. Rounded knotty depression in the centre of a person's belly caused by the detachment of the umbilical cord after birth; the umbilicus. **2.** The central point of a place.

- **Nay:** No; a negative answer.
  Neigh: A horse's cry.
- **None:** Not any; no one.
  Nun: Member of a female religious community (usually Christian), living under vows of chastity, obedience and poverty.

****

O

- **Oar:** A pole with a flat blade that is used to row or steer a boat through the water.
  Ore: Naturally occurring solid material from which a metal or valuable mineral can be extracted.
- **Oh:** An exclamation of surprise or interjection.
  Owe: 1. Have an obligation to pay money or goods to someone in return for something received. **2.** To be under a moral obligation to show gratitude, respect etc. or to offer an explanation to someone.
- **Ordinance:** An authoritative order.
  Ordnance: 1. Mounted guns or cannons. **2.** A government department dealing especially with military stores and materials.
- **Our:** Belonging to or associated with the speaker and one or more persons previously mentioned or easily identified.
  Hour: 1. Period of time equal to a twenty-fourth part of a day and night and divided into 60 minutes. **2.** A time of day specified as an exact number of hours from midnight or midday. **3.** Period set aside for a particular purpose or marked by a specific activity (e.g., *work hours* or *leisure hours*).
- **Overdo:** To use too much of; exaggerate.
  Overdue: Past the time when due or scheduled; not having arrived, been born etc. at the expected time

****

P

- **Pail:** A bucket.

    Pale: 1. Containing little colour or pigment; light in colour; (a person's face) having little colour, usually due to shock, fear or ill health. **2.** Unimpressive or inferior (*a pale imitation*). **3.** Seem or become less important (*to pale in comparison*). **4.** A wooden stake used with others to form a fence. **5.** A boundary (*lie outside the pale of morality*).

- **Pain: 1.** Strong unpleasant and hurting bodily sensation such as one caused by illness or injury. **2.** Mental suffering or distress.

    Pane: 1. A single sheet of glass in a window or door. **2.** A sheet or page of stamps.

- **Pair:** A set of two.

    Pare: 1. Trim by cutting away the edges. **2.** Reduce or diminish in a number of small successive stages.

    Pear: A yellowish- or brownish-green edible fruit; the tree that bears this fruit.

- **Palate: 1.** The roof of the mouth, separating the cavities of the mouth and nose in vertebrates. **2.** A person's ability to distinguish between and appreciate different flavours. **3.** The flavour of a wine or beer.

    Palette: 1. A thin board or other surface on which an artist lays and mixes colours. **2.** The range of colours used by a particular artist or at a particular time. **3.** The range or variety of tonal or instrumental colour in a musical piece.

    Pallet: 1. A straw mattress. **2.** A crude or makeshift bed. **3.** A portable platform on which goods can be moved, stacked and stored. **4.** A flat wooden blade with a handle that is used to shape clay or plaster.

- **Pause:** A temporary stop in action or speech.

    Paws: 1. An animal's foot having claws and pads. **2.** (Informal) A person's hand.

- **Pea:** A round green seed eaten as a vegetable; the leguminous plant which yields pods containing peas.

    Pee: 1. To urinate. **2.** Urine.

- **Peak: 1.** The pointed top of a mountain. **2.** A point in a curve or on a graph. **3.** The point of highest activity or achievement.
  Peek: 1. To look quickly or furtively. **2.** Protrude slightly so as to be just visible.
  Pique: 1. A feeling of irritation or resentment resulting from a slight, particularly to one's pride. **2.** Stimulate one's interest or curiosity.

- **Peal: 1.** Loud ringing of bell(s). **2.** A loud repeated or reverberating sound of thunder or laughter.
  Peel: 1. Remove the outer covering or skin from a fruit or vegetable. **2.** The outer covering or skin of a fruit or vegetable.

- **Pedal: 1.** Each of a pair of foot-operated levers for moving a bicycling or other vehicle propelled by leg power. **2.** To move (a bicycle, tricycle etc.) by working the pedals.
  Peddle: 1. Sell goods (especially small items) by going from place to place. **2.** Sell (an illegal drug or stolen item). **3.** (Derogatory) Promote an idea or view persistently.

- **Plain: 1.** Simple and ordinary, not decorated or elaborate. **2.** Easy to perceive or understand.
  Plane: 1. A flat surface on which a straight line joining any two points would wholly lie. **2.** Completely level or flat. **3.** A level of existence or thought.

- **Pray: 1.** Address a prayer to god or another deity. **2.** Wish or hope earnestly for a specific outcome.
  Prey: 1. An animal hunted and killed by another for food. **2.** Hunt and kill for food. **3.** Exploit or injure; cause trouble to.

- **Principal: 1.** First in order of importance; main. **2.** Denoting an original sum of money invested or lent. **3.** The head of a school or college. **4.** (Law) A person directly responsible for a crime (the *principal* accused).
  Principle: 1. A fundamental truth or proposition serving as the foundation for belief or action. **2.** Morally correct behaviour and attitude. **3.** A fundamental source or basis for something. **4.** (Chemistry) An active or characteristic constituent of a substance.

****

- **Quarts:** Several units of liquid capacity equal to a quarter of a gallon or two pints, equivalent in Britain to approximately 1.13 litres and in the US to approximately 0.94 litres.

  Quartz: A hard mineral consisting of silica, typically occurring as colourless or white hexagonal prisms.

- **Queue:** A line or sequence of people or vehicles awaiting their turn to be attended to or to proceed.

  Cue: A signal or prompt for action.

****

- **Rain: 1.** The condensed moisture of the atmosphere falling visibly to earth in separate drops. **2.** A large quantity of things falling or descending.

  Reign: 1. To rule as a monarch or king. **2.** The period of rule of a monarch. **3.** The period during which someone or something is predominant or pre-eminent.

  Rein: 1. A long, narrow strap attached at one end to a horse's bit, typically used in pairs to guide or check a horse in riding or driving. **2.** To check or guide a horse by tugging on its reins. **3.** (**Reins**) The power to direct and control.

- **Raise: 1.** Lift or move to a higher position or level. **2.** Construct or build (a structure). **3.** Increase the amount, level or strength of; promote to a higher rank. **4.** Cause to be heard, felt or considered. **5.** Generate (a bill, invoice etc.). **6.** Collect or levy (money or resources). **7.** Bring up (a child). **8.** Breed or grow (animals or plants). **9.** Wake from sleep or bring back from death. **10.** Abandon or force to abandon (a blockade, embargo, siege).

  Raze: Tear down and destroy (a building, town, village, etc.).

- **Rap:** A sharp knock; to strike with a series of rapid audible blows.

  Wrap: 1. Cover or enclose in paper or soft material. **2.** (Informal) Finish or conclude something.

- **Read:** To look at and comprehend the meaning of written or printed matter by interpreting the character or symbols of which it is composed; speak aloud (written or printed words).
  Reed: A tall, slender-leaved plant of the grass family that grows in water or on marshy ground.

- **Roe: 1.** The mass of eggs contained in the ovaries of a female fish or shellfish, especially when ripe and used as food. **2.** A small deer with a reddish summer coat that turns greyish in winter.
  Row: 1. A number of people or things in a more or less straight line. **2.** Propel a boat with oars. **3.** (Informal) A heated quarrel. **4.** A loud noise or uproar.

- **Root:** A temporary stop in action or speech.
  Route: A way or course taken in getting from a starting point to a destination; a path of travel.

- **Rot: 1.** Decompose by action of bacteria and fungi, decay. **2.** The process of decaying. **3.** Gradually deteriorate or decline.
  Wrought: (Of metals) Beaten out or shaped by hammering.

- **Rote:** Mechanical or habitual repetition.
  Wrote: Has written, past tense of *write*.

- **Rude:** Impolite, without manners and a sense of etiquette.
  Rued: Regretted, to have felt sorry about.

****

S

- **Sachet:** A small sealed bag or packet containing a limited quantity of something.
  Sashay: 1. Walk ostentatiously, with exaggerated hip and shoulder movements. **2.** Perform the sashay.

- **Seam:** A line where two pieces of fabric are sewn together in a garment or other article.
  Seem: Give the impression of being.

- **Sear: 1.** Burn or scorch with sudden intense heat. **2.** (Of pain) Be experienced as a sudden burning sensation.

Seer: 1. A person of supposed supernatural insight who sees visions of the future. **2.** An enlightened person or one who has attained *nirvana*. **3.** A varying unit of weight (about one kilogram) or liquid measure (about one litre), used in the Indian subcontinent.

- **Serf:** (During feudal times) An agricultural labourer who was bonded to working on a particular estate.
  Surf: 1. The mass or line of foam formed by waves breaking on a seashore or reef. **2.** Stand or lie on a surfboard and ride on the crest of a wave towards the shore. **3.** To be occupied by moving from one website to another on the Internet.

- **Shear: 1.** To cut the wool off a sheep or other animal. **2.** Break off or cause to break off, owing to a structural strain.
  Sheer: 1. Nothing other than, unmitigated (*sheer* bad luck). **2.** Perpendicular or nearly so (of a cliff, wall, etc.). **3.** Very thin (of a fabric). **4.** Swerve or change course quickly (especially a boat).

- **Sic:** Written exactly as it appears in the original (used after a copied or quoted word).
  Sick: 1. Affected by physical or mental illness. **2.** Feeling nauseous or wanting to vomit. **3.** Bored, weary or tired of (especially through excessive exposure). **4.** (Of humour) Dealing offensively with unpleasant or upsetting subjects. **5.** Having abnormal or unnatural tendencies (especially sexual).

- **Slay:** To kill or murder someone.
  Sleigh: A sledge drawn by horses or reindeer; to ride on a sleigh.

- **Soar: 1.** Fly or rise high into the air. **2.** Increase rapidly above the usual level.
  Sore: 1. Painful or aching. **2.** Upset and angry. **3.** Severe, urgent.

- **Sole: 1.** The underside of a person's foot. **2.** The underside of a tool or implement. **3.** One and only.
  Soul: 1. The spiritual or immaterial part of a human, regarded as immortal. **2.** A person who is regarded as the embodiment of some quality.

- **Stake:** A wooden pole
  Steak: A slice of meat.

- **Stationary: 1.** Not moving. **2.** Not changing in quantity or condition.
  Stationery: Paper or other materials needed for writing.

- **Storey:** A floor or part of a building comprising all the rooms that are on the same level.
  Story: 1. An account of imaginary or real people and events told for entertainment. **2.** An account of past events, experiences, etc. **3.** (Informal) A lie.

- **Succour:** Assistance and support in times of hardship and distress.
  Sucker: (Informal) A gullible person or one whom it is easy to deceive.

- **Suite:** A set of rooms for one person's or family's use or for a particular purpose, especially in a hotel.
  Sweet: 1. With the pleasant taste characteristic of sugar or honey; not salty, sour or bitter. **2.** (Of air, water, etc.) Fresh, pure, untainted. **3.** Pleasing in general, delightful. **4.** (Of a person) Pleasant and kind or thoughtful. **5.** A small shaped piece of confectionary made of sugar. **6.** A sweet dish forming a course of a meal; a pudding or dessert.

- **Sundae:** A dish of ice cream with added such as fruit, nuts and syrup or chocolate.
  Sunday: The day of the week before Monday and after Saturday, observed by Christians as a day of rest and religious worship.

- **Symbol: 1.** A thing that represents or stands for something else, especially a material object representing something abstract. **2.** A mark or character used as a conventional representation of something.
  Cymbal: A musical instrument consisting of a slightly concave round brass plate that is either struck against one or struck with a stick.

****

T

- **Taught:** Past tense of *teach*.
  Taut: 1. Stretched or pulled tight. **2.** (Of writing, music, etc.) Concise and controlled. **3.** (Of a ship) Having a disciplined crew.

- **Team: 1.** A group of players forming one side in a competitive game or sport. **2.** Two or more people working together.
  Teem: Be full of or swarming with.
- **Throne:** A ceremonial chair for a monarch, bishop or similar figure.
  Thrown: To be hurled.
- **Tic:** A habitual spasmodic contraction of the muscles, most often in the face.
  Tick: 1. A mark (✓) that indicates a textual item is correct or has been checked or chosen. **2.** A regular short, sharp sound, especially that made every second by a clock or watch. **3.** A parasitic arachnid that attaches itself to the skin, from where it sucks blood. **4.** (Informal) A worthless or contemptible person.
- **Tighten:** To make tighter or better fitting.
  Titan: 1. Any member of a family of giant gods in Greek mythology. **2.** A person or thing of great strength, intellect or importance.
- **Timber:** Wood meant for use in building and carpentry.
  Timbre: The character or quality of a musical sound or voice as distinct from its pitch and intensity.
- **Troop: 1.** A soldiers or members of the armed forces. **2.** A cavalry unit commanded by a captain. **3.** A group of people or animals of a particular kind.
  Troupe: A group of dancers, actors or other entertains who move from place to place performing at different venues.

****

U

- **Urn: 1.** A tall, rounded vase with a stem and base, especially one for storing a cremated person's ashes. **2.** A large metal container with a tap, in which tea or coffee is made and kept hot.
  Earn: Obtain (money) in return for labour or services; gain (money) as interest or profit (of capital invested).
- **Use:** Treat in a particular manner; take, hold or employ as a means of accomplishing something.
  Ewes: Female sheep.

****

- **Vain: 1.** A person who has or shows an excessively high opinion of his/her appearance and abilities. **2.** Useless.

  Vein: 1. Any of the tubes forming a part of the circulatory system by which blood is conveyed to all parts of the body towards the heart. **2.** In plants, a slender rib that forms part of the supporting framework of a wing. **3.** A distinctive quality, style or tendency (*he was speaking in a humorous vein*).

- **Vale:** A valley.

  Veil: 1. A fine material worn to protect or conceal, particularly used by women. **2.** A thing that conceals, disguises or obscures.

- **Verses: 1.** Writing that is arranged in a metrical rhythm. **2.** A group of lines that form a unit in a poem or song. **3.** Each of the short numbered divisions of a chapter in the Bible or other scriptures.

  Versus: Against, as opposed to, in contrast to (especially used in sporting and legal context).

****

- **Wade:** Walk through any liquid or viscous substance.

  Weighed: To have one's weight taken.

- **Wail:** A prolonged and high-pitched cry of pain, grief or anger; let out or utter a wail.

  Wale: 1. A ridge on a textured woven fabric such as corduroy. **2.** A horizontal band around a woven basket. **3.** (Nautical) A horizontal wooden strip fitted to strengthen a boat's side.

  Whale: A very large marine mammal and the largest creatures on earth.

- **Waist: 1.** The part of the human body that lies below the ribs and above the hips. **2.** The narrow portion in the middle of something.

  Waste: 1. To use carelessly, extravagantly or without specific purpose. **2.** Be unable to make proper or good use of. **3.** To become progressively weaker and thinner (*to waste away*).

- **Waive:** To refrain from insisting upon or enforcing/applying a right or claim.
  Wave: 1. To move the hand to and fro in greeting or as a signal. **2.** Style hair so that it curls slightly. **3.** A ridge of water curling into an arched form and breaking on the shore or between two depressions in open water. **4.** A sudden occurrence of or increase in a specified phenomenon or emotion.
- **Want:** To have a desire to do or possess something.
  Wont: Accustomed to, one's customary behaviour or habit.
- **Wet: 1.** Covered or saturated with a liquid. **2.** (Of paint, ink, etc.) Not yet dry or hardened. **3.** (British, informal) Lacking forcefulness or strength of character. **4.** (Informal, of an area) Allowing the free sale of alcoholic drinks.
  Whet: 1. To sharpen the blade of a tool or weapon. **2.** To excite or stimulate (a person's desire, interest or appetite).
- **Whine: 1.** A long, high-pitched complaining cry. **2.** A feeble or petulant complaint. **3.** To complain in a feeble or petulant manner.
  Wine: An alcoholic drink that's made from fermented grape juice.
- **Who's:** A contraction of *who is* or *who has*.
  Whose: (Interrogative) Belonging to or associated with which person.

****

X

- **Xi:** The fourteenth letter of the Greek alphabet, transliterated as 'x'.
  Psi: 1. The twenty-third letter of the Greek alphabet, transliterated as 'ps'. **2.** Supposed para-psychological or psychic faculties or phenomena.

****

Y

- **Yack:** A variant spelling of *Yak* – denoting a trivial or unduly persistent conversation (*informal*).

  Yak: A large ox with shaggy hair, humped shoulders and large horns that is used in Tibet as a pack animal and also for its meat, milk and hide.

- **Yoke: 1.** A wooden crosspiece fastened over the necks of two animals and attached to a plough or cart that they pull together. **2.** A frame fitted over the neck or shoulders of a person, used for carrying pails or baskets.

- **Yolk:** The internal yellow part of a bird's egg.

Foreign Words in English

The English language is rightly called *the greatest borrower of the world*. Many English words have been borrowed from Latin, Greek, French, Spanish, German, Portuguese and our very own Sanskrit and Hindi. In this chapter, we will concentrate on words derived from foreign languages, including some of Indian origin.

Ad nauseam (Latin): Something that's done to a sickening, disgusting or tiresomely excessive degree.

Aegis (Greek): The protection, patronage, backing or support of someone.

Aficionado (Spanish): A devoted follower of a sport, a fan, an amateur, a person who is very knowledgeable or enthusiastic about a subject.

Agent provocateur (French): A person employed (say, by a company) with the specific purpose of joining a group (for instance, a trade union) or political party etc. to pretend sympathy with their cause and thereby incite them to commit acts for which they could be punished or convicted.

Alter ego (Latin): **1.** A person's secondary or alternative personality. **2.** A close friend who is much like oneself.

Amnesty (Greek): An official pardon granted by the authorities for people who are convicted of political offences; an undertaking by the authorities to take no action against specified offences during a fixed period.

Amok/Amuck (Malay): Behave in an uncontrollable or disruptive fashion.

Angst (German): Dread; a feeling of anxiety.

Apartheid (Dutch, Afrikaans): A policy of segregation or discrimination between races that was prevalent in South Africa (1948-1991).

Aperitif (French): An alcoholic drink that's taken before meals to stimulate the appetite.

Armada (Spanish): A fleet of warships.

Avant-garde (French): New and unusual or experimental (especially in the arts).

Avatar (Sanskrit): A manifestation of a god or deity on earth in bodily form (chiefly in Hinduism).

Avuncular (Latin): Like an uncle (in being kind and friendly towards a younger or less experienced person).

****

Bandicoot (Telugu): An Asian rat that is a destructive pest in many places.

Bete noire (French): A person or thing one particularly dislikes or hates.

Bona fide (Latin): In good faith, genuine, real, without any intention to deceive.

Bonanza (Spanish): A source of wealth, good fortune or profits.

Boondocks (Tagalog): Rough or isolated country; wilderness, backwoods or the jungle.

Bravura (Italian): A show of daring or brilliance.

****

Canard (French): An unfounded rumour; a silly or absurd story.

Carte blanche (French): Complete freedom to act or do as one thinks best.

Cause celebre (French): A controversial issue that attracts a great deal of public attention.

Chauffeur (French): A person employed to drive a car, usually in uniform.

Cheroot (Tamil): A cigar that has both ends open.

Chutzpah (Yiddish): Shameless audacity.

Cornucopia (Latin): **1.** An abundant supply of good things. **2.** A goat's horn overflowing with flowers, fruit and corn, which was a symbol of plenty, according to legend.

Coup de grace (French): A sudden, violent seizure of power from a government; a sudden stroke of state policy.

Coup d'etat (French): Literally, "a blow of mercy"; a final, decisive blow or stroke (given to kill a wounded person or animal).

Cul-de-sac (French): A blind alley; a dead end.

****

Debacle (French): An utter failure or disaster.

De facto (Latin): In fact, whether by right or not; in reality; functioning.

Déjà vu (French): A feeling of already having been to a place or having experienced the situation before.

Dekko (Hindi): A quick look or glance (informal, British usage).

Demarche (French): A step or course of action, particularly in politics and diplomacy, that often marks a change of policy.

De rigueur (French): Required by etiquette or current fashion.

Desperado (Spanish): A desperate or reckless criminal.

Détente (French): The easing or relaxation of tensions or strained relations between governments or countries.

Dilettante (Italian): A person who cultivates a particular interest (for instance, the arts) without real knowledge or commitment; a dabbler; one with an amateurish or superficial interest.

Double entendre (French): A word or phrase that can be interpreted in two ways, one of which is usually indecent or vulgar.

Dramatis personae (Latin): The cast or characters of a play, novel or narrative; the chief actors in a dramatic series of events.

****

Echelon (French): A level or rank in an organisation.

Elan (French): Energy, style and enthusiasm.

Enfant terrible (French): A person who behaves in an unconventional, controversial or embarrassing way; a child whose words cause embarrassment.

En masse (French): In a body; all together.

Ersatz (German): A substitute; synthetic; inferior; a shoddy product; not the real thing.

Ethos (Greek): The characteristic spirit of a culture, era or community that is revealed in its attitudes and aspirations.

Etiquette (French): The customary code of polite or politically correct behaviour in society.

Ex officio (Latin): By virtue of one's office, position or status.

****

Fait accompli (French): A thing that has been done or decided, leaving those affected by it with no option but to accept it.

Faux pas (French): A social blunder, a glaring mistake.

Femme fatale (French): An attractive and seductive woman; a woman who leads men to their death and destruction.

Fetish (Portuguese): Something for which a person has a blind, illogical affection.

****

Gaffe (French): An embarrassing blunder.

Graffiti (Italian): Unauthorised writings or drawings on a surface in a public place.

Gung-ho (Chinese): Unthinkingly enthusiastic an eager, especially about taking part in fighting or warfare.

Gusto (Spanish): Enjoyment or vigour.

****

Haute couture (French): The designing and making of high-quality fashionable clothes by leading fashion houses.

Hoi polloi (Greek): The common people (usually used in the derogatory sense).

Hors d'oeuvre (French): A savoury appetiser.

****

Imbroglio (Italian): A violent and complicated quarrel; an embarrassing and painful misunderstanding.

Incommunicado (Spanish): Without means of communication; deprived of contact with the outside world, particularly a person held in solitary confinement.

In extremis (Latin): **1.** In an extremely difficult situation. **2.** At the point of death.

Inter alia (Latin): Among other things.

In toto (Latin): As a whole; entirely; in full.

****

Junta (Spanish): A council or committee; a secret council; a group of plotters.

****

Kowtow (Chinese): To be excessively subservient and servile towards someone.

Kudos (Greek): Praise and honour.

****

Laissez-faire (French): A policy of non-interference, especially abstention by governments from interfering in the workings of the free market.

Lingua franca (Italian): A common language; any common language used by peoples of different tongues to enable them to understand each other.

Largesse (French): **1.** Generosity. **2.** Money or gifts that are given generously.

****

Macabre (French): Disturbing or horrifying, especially something concerned with death and injury.

Maelstrom (Dutch): **1.** A powerful whirlpool. **2.** A scene of confused movement or upheaval.

Maestro (Italian): **1.** A distinguished conductor or performer of classical music. **2.** A distinguished figure in any field.

Magnum opus (Latin): A large and important work of art, music or literature, particularly a work considered the most important one of an artist, writer or other specialist.

Mandarin (Chinese): A powerful official or senior bureaucrat.

Minion (French): A follower or underling of a powerful person (e.g. a politician), particularly a servile and unimportant one.

Modus operandi (Latin): A way of doing something; the way in which something works.

Mogul (Persian): An important or powerful person (informal).

****

Noblesse oblige (French): Privilege entails responsibility; benevolent, honourable behaviour that is considered to be the responsibility of persons of high birth or rank.

Nom de plume (French): A pen name; a pseudonym.

****

Pariah (Tamil): An outcast; a member of a low caste in southern India.

Peccadillo (Spanish): A minor sin or fault.

Per se (Latin): By or in itself; intrinsically.

Persona non grata (Latin): A person who is unacceptable or unwelcome.

Piece de resistance (French): The chief item or most important feature of a creative work or meal etc.; the main dish or course.

Potpourri (French): A mixture of things, a medley, a mishmash.

Presto (Italian): Announcing the successful completion of a conjuring trick or other surprising achievement.

Prima facie (Latin): At first sight, accepted as so until proved otherwise (law).

Pronto (Spanish): Quickly; rapidly.

Putsch (German): A petty rebellion or popular uprising; a violent attempt to overthrow a government.

****

Quid pro quo (Latin): Something for something, a favour or advantage given in return for something.

Qui vive (French): Derived from a sentry's challenge of "Who goes there?"; on the alert; to be on the lookout.

****

Raison d'etre (French): The reason for being; the reason for the existence of some action or policy; justification.

Rapprochement (French): The establishment or resumption of cordial relations; to draw closer together.

Realpolitik (German): Politics based on practical considerations, rather than moral, ethical or ideological ones.

Riposte (French): A quick clever reply.

****

Sangfroid (French): Composure or coolness under pressure and trying circumstances.

Satrap (Persian): A subordinate or local ruler.

Savoir faire (French): An instinctive ability to act appropriately in a specific situation.

Sine qua non (Latin): A thing that is absolutely essential.

Sotto voce (Italian): In a quiet voice; privately; in an undertone or whisper.

Status quo (Latin): The existing state of affairs.

Status quo ante (Latin): The previous state of affairs.

Strafe (German): Attack with machine-gun fire or bombs from low-flying aircraft.

****

Tete-a-tete (French): A private conversation between two persons.

Tour de force (French): A performance or achievement accomplished with great skill.

Tycoon (Japanese): A wealthy, powerful person in business or industry.

****

Vendetta (Italian): **1.** A blood feud in which the family of a murdered person seeks vengeance on the killer or the killer's family. **2.** A prolonged bitter quarrel or a campaign against someone.

Vignette (French): **1.** A brief evocative description, account or episode. **2.** A small illustration or portrait-photograph which fades into its background without a definite border.

Virtuoso (Italian): **1.** A person highly skilled in music or another artistic pursuit. **2.** A person with special knowledge of or interest in works of art or curios.

Volte-face (French): An about-face; a complete turnabout, a reversal of policy, opinion or attitude.

Vox populi (Latin): The beliefs or opinions of the majority of people.

****

Wunderkind (German): Wonder child; a prodigy; an extremely talented youngster.

****

Zeitgeist (German): The mood of the times; the defining spirit of a particular period.

∞

Slang and Rhyming Language

Rhyming words are more often than not slang terms. However, they have a charm and romance all their own. Here are some select rhyming words.

Airy-fairy
Adj. *Informal.* Foolishly idealistic and vague; not realistic; impractical; visionary.
Example: Emperor Mohammed Bin Tughlak always came up with *airy-fairy* schemes that depleted his treasury.

Bigwig
N. *Informal.* An important and influential person.
Example: There are many *bigwigs* in South Delhi.

Boo-boo
N. *Informal.* A foolish or silly mistake; blunder.
Example: He committed quite a few *boo-boos* in the exams.

Boogie-woogie
N. *Informal.* A dance to pop or rock music.
Example: On New Year's eve, teenagers love to *boogie-woogie* into the late hours of the night.

Brain drain
N. *Informal.* The emigration of highly skilled or qualified people from a region or country.
Example: For decades, India suffered a severe *brain drain* when her most skilled citizens migrated to the States.

Bric-a-brac
N. Miscellaneous objects and ornaments of little value.
Example: Many designers fill their homes with *bric-a-brac*.

****

Chit-chat
N. *Informal.* Inconsequential conversation; light, informal talk; gossip.
V. Talk about trivial matters.
Example: Girls are very fond of *chit-chat*.

Chock-a-block
Adj. *Informal.* Crammed full or tightly.
Example: Harshad Mehta's suitcase was *chock-a-block* with currency notes.

Chow chow
N. *Informal.*
1. A mixed vegetable pickle, primarily made by Chinese.
2. A Chinese preserve of ginger, orange peel and other ingredients in syrup.
3. Another term for **chow**, slang (chiefly American) for food or mealtimes.
Example: Let's have some *chow chow*.

Claptrap
N. Nonsense; showy, insincere, empty talk or writing, intended only to get applause or attention.
Example: As a film star, Shatrughan Sinha was full of *clap-trap*.

Culture vulture
N. *Informal.* A person who is very interested in culture and the arts.
Example: Although unlettered, Emperor Akbar was renowned as a *culture vulture*.

****

Dilly-dally
V. Dawdle or vacillate; to waste time in hesitation.
Example: Saddam Hussein kept *dilly-dallying* with all UN requests for an arms inspection.

Ding-dong
N. *Informal.* A fierce argument or fight.
Adj. Evenly matched or intensely waged (contest or fight).
Example: The legendary King Kong and Dara Singh fought *ding-dong* bouts in the 1950s and 1960s.

Dodo
N. A large extinct flightless bird formerly found in Mauritius.
Informal. A foolish or stupid person; an old-fashioned person; a dullard.
Example: Some politicians act like *dodos* (or *dodoes*).
Phrase: As dead as a dodo.

Downtown
Adj., Adv. Of, in, like or towards the central area or main business area of a city or town.
N. Such an area of a city or town.
Example: Colaba and Cuffe Parade are Mumbai's *downtown* areas.

Dribs and drabs
Pl. N. *Informal.* In small scattered or sporadic amounts.
Example: The NGO received foreign aid *in dribs and drabs*.
Phrase: In dribs and drabs.

Dum-dum
N. *Informal.* A stupid person.
Example: Comedians are paid to act like *dum-dums*.

****

Fag hag
N. *Informal. Derogatory.* A heterosexual woman who spends much of her time with homosexual men.
Example: Some women feel safer being *fag hags*.

Flip-flop
N. 1. An acrobatic spring backward from the feet to the hands and back to the feet. *Informal.* **2.** An abrupt reversal of policy.
Example: Pakistan's policy towards terrorism is a series of *flip-flops*.

Flotsam and jetsam
N. *Phrase.*
   1. The wreckage of a ship or its cargo floating at sea.

2. Useless or discarded objects; odds and ends.

3. Unemployed people who drift from place to place.

Example: At high tide, the sea is usually full of *flotsam and jetsam*.

Flower power

N. The promotion of peace and love by the hippies as a means of changing the world.

Example: *Flower power* ruled the roost in the late 60s and early 70s.

Frou-frou (fru-fru)

N. 1. A rustling or swishing noise made by someone walking in a dress.

    2. Frills or other ornamentation, particularly of women's clothes.

    3. *Informal.* Excessive ornateness or affected elegance.

Example: Girls are fond of *frou-frou* skirts.

Fuddy-duddy

N. *Informal.*

    1. A person who is very old-fashioned and pompous.

    2. A fussy, critical person.

Example: Some elderly persons become *fuddy-duddies* after the age of 65.

****

Gaga

Adj. *Informal.*

    1. Slightly mad, especially as a result of old age.

    2. Mentally confused, crazy.

    3. Carried away, as by love or enthusiasm.

Example: MF Husain goes *gaga* when talking about Madhuri Dixit.

****

Hanky-panky

N. 1. *Humorous.* Behaviour considered improper, but not seriously so.

    2. *Informal.* Trickery or deception, especially in connection with shady dealings or illicit sexual activity.

Example: Amitabh Bachchan does not like any *hanky-panky* on the sets.

Harum-scarum
Adj. Acting or done in a reckless, impetuous, rash, or irresponsible manner.
Example: Salman Khan is notorious for his *harum-scarum* deeds.

Heebie-jeebies
Pl. N. A state of nervous fear or anxiety (used with *the*).
Example: Most prisoners on death row are overcome by *the heebie-jeebies*.

Helter-skelter
Adj. & **Adv.** In disorderly haste or confusion.
Example: During the Kumbh Mela stampede, devotees ran *helter-skelter*.

Heyday
N. The period of one's greatest success, prosperity, activity or vigour.
Example: Reliance Industries is enjoying its *heyday*.

Higgledy-piggledy
Adv. In jumbled confusion or disorder.
Adj. Disorderly; jumbled; confused.
Example: When Saddam Hussein was captured, the deposed dictator seemed to be in a *higgledy-piggledy* state.

Hillbilly
N. *Informal.* An unsophisticated rural person; usually a contemptuous term.
Example: People from some north Indian states are considered to be hillbillies.

Hobnob
V. *Informal.* Mix socially, especially with those of higher social status.
Example: Samajwadi Party leader Amar Singh is known for *hobnobbing* with the rich and famous.

Hobo
N. 1. A vagrant or tramp.
   2. A migratory worker (chiefly American).
Example: During the Great Depression of the 1930s, America had many *hobos* (or *hoboes*).

Hotchpotch
N. 1. A confused mixture.

   2. *Archaic*. A mutton stew with mixed vegetables.

Example: When in a rush to go to office, most bachelors end up cooking some *hotchpotch*.

Hocus-pocus
N. 1. Meaningless talk used for trickery.

   2. A form of words used by magicians.

Example: Conmen are very good at *hocus-pocus*.

Hoi polloi
Pl. N. *Derogatory*. The common people; the masses (sometimes preceded by *the*).

Example: Soviet dictator Josef Stalin never bothered about *the hoi polloi*.

Hoity-toity
Adj. Haughty; arrogant; condescending.

Example: Sridevi has essayed many *hoity-toity* roles in Hindi films.

Hoodoo
N. 1. Voodoo.

   2. Bad luck.

   3. A person or thing that causes bad luck.

Example: *Hoodoo* is considered a way of life in Haiti.

(By) Hook or by crook
Phrase. By any possible means, honest or dishonest.

Example: Pakistan wanted to join the Nuclear Club *by hook or by crook*.

Hubbub
N. 1. A chaotic din caused by a crowd.

   2. A busy noisy situation.

   3. Uproar, tumult.

Example: When India beat Pakistan in the One Day series, there was a *hubbub* throughout Pakistan.

Huff and puff
V. 1. Blow out noisily; breathe heavily.
   2. Perform a task with great difficulty.
Example: Even minor tasks would make Hardy *huff and puff*.

Humdrum
Adj. Lacking variety; dull; monotonous; boring.
N. Monotonous routine.
Example: Life in small cities is sometimes very *humdrum*.

Humpty-dumpty
N. *Informal.*
   1. A short fat person.
   2. A person or thing that cannot be restored, once overthrown.
Example: Many dictators are *humpty-dumpty* characters.

Hunky-dory
Adj. *Informal.* Excellent; fine.
Example: The relationship between the United States and India now seems *hunky-dory*.

Hurly-burly
N. Busy, boisterous activity; uproar; confusion.
Adj. Disorderly and confused.
Example: In the *hurly-burly* of office life, you must learn to keep your cool.

Hush-hush
Adj. *Informal.* Highly secret or confidential.
Example: Working as an undercover agent requires a person to lead a *hush-hush* life.

Hustle and bustle
N. Excited, hurried activity and movement.
V. Move energetically, hurriedly and noisily.
Example: In Mumbai, there is a lot of *hustle and bustle*.

****

Ipso facto
Adv. By that very fact or act (the word is usually written in italics, due to its Latin origins).
Example: Considering the circumstantial evidence, the court ruled that he was guilty of the crime *ipso facto*.

Itsy-bitsy
Adj. *Informal.* Very small.
Example: Bollywood actress Kareena Kapoor is fond of wearing *itsy-bitsy* outfits.

****

Jet set
N. *Informal.* Wealthy people who travel by air widely and frequently for business or pleasure.
Example: Delhi and Mumbai have most of the *jet set* people in India.

****

Knick-knack
N. *Informal.* A small worthless object, especially an ornament.
Example: Small children are always attracted to *knick-knacks*.

Kowtow
V. 1. *Historical.* Kneel and touch the ground with the forehead in submission as part of Chinese custom.
   2. Be excessively subservient towards someone.
Example: V. Prabhakaran wants all Tamil groups in Lanka to *kowtow* to his policies.

****

Lowbrow
Adj. *Informal. Chiefly derogatory.* Not highly intellectual or cultured.
Example: People who do not attend school end up being *lowbrow* individuals.

****

Mayday
N. An international radio distress signal used by ships and aircraft.
Example: *Mayday* signals only caught on after the sinking of the Titanic.

Mishmash
N. A confused mixture.
Example: A good chef will never recommend *mishmash* recipes.

Mumbo-jumbo
N. *Informal.* Words or ritual causing or intended to cause confusion or bewilderment; meaningless ritual.
Example: Many god-men use *mumbo-jumbo* to fool their disciples.

****

Namby-pamby
Adj. *Derogatory.* Lacking courage or vigour; feeble; weakly sentimental.
Example: Many ministers in Indira Gandhi's Cabinet were *namby-pamby* characters.

Nitty-gritty
N. *Informal.* The most important aspects or practical details of a matter.
Example: India and Pakistan will have to look into the *nitty-gritty* of all major issues.

Nitwit
N. *Informal.* A silly or foolish person.
Example: In Hindi films of the 1960s, Rajendranath played the role of a *nitwit* to perfection.

****

Pell-mell
Adj. & **Adv.** In a confused, rushed or disorderly manner.
N. A confused mixture; disorder.
Example: When the earthquake struck Bhuj, people ran *pell-mell*.

Powwow
N. 1. North American Red Indian ceremony involving feasting and dancing.
   2. *Informal.* A meeting for discussion among friends or colleagues.
Example: The Indian cricketers held a *powwow* to discuss the security implications of a Pakistan tour.

****

Ragtag
Adj. Untidy or disorganised; made up of mixed or ill-sorted elements.
Example: In his early years, Genghis Khan led a *ragtag* army and yet he finally succeeded in carving the world's largest empire.

Razzmatazz
N. *Informal.* Rowdy, showy and exciting activity and display.
Example: All Goan festivals are famous for their *razzmatazz*.

Riff-raff
N. 1. Disreputable or undesirable people; rabble.
   2. Worthless stuff.
Example: Asia's largest slum, Dharavi in Mumbai, is known for its riff-raff elements.

Roly-poly
Adj. *Informal.* Round and plump.
Example: Yesteryears' comedienne Tun Tun's *roly-poly* frame evoked considerable mirth among film audiences.

****

Sanctum sanctorum
N. 1. The holy of holies in the Jewish temple.
   2. A place of utmost inviolability and privacy.
Example: When devotees enter the *sanctum sanctorum* they maintain pin-drop silence.

Shilly-shally
V. Be indecisive.
N. Indecisive behaviour.
Example: *Shilly-shally* people don't go very far in life.

Shipshape
Adj. Orderly and neat.
Example: As a designer, one's work must always be *shipshape*.

Summum bonum
N. The highest or supreme good, especially as the ultimate goal according to which values and priorities are established in an ethical system (usually written in italics).

Example: Truth is the *summum bonum* of all religions.

****

Ticky-tacky
N. *Informal.* Inferior, shoddy or cheap material, especially as used in suburban constructions.
Example: DDA flats in Delhi are noted for their *ticky-tacky* work.

Titbit
N. 1. A small piece of tasty food.
    2. A small and interesting item of gossip or information.
Example: Film magazines like Stardust come up with spicy *titbits* month after month.

True-blue
Adj. Extremely loyal (to a cause or party) or orthodox.
Example: A few veteran politicians are *true-blue* Congressmen.

****

Voodoo
N. 1. A religion of West Indies, especially Haiti, based on beliefs and practices of African and Roman Catholic origin and noted for its interests in sorcery, charms and fetishes.
    2. A person who practices voodoo.
Adj. *Informal.*
    3. Claimed or reputed to provide an ingenious or seemingly magical solution to a problem, but in reality of little value or effectiveness.
Example: *Voodoo* is still practised in some West Indies islands.

****

Wacky backy
N. (*British, informal*) Cannabis.
Example: Have you ever tried any *wacky backy*?

Walkie-talkie
N. A portable two-way radio.
Example: *Walkie-talkies* are standard equipment in all police vans.

Willy-nilly

Adv. 1. Whether one likes it or not.

    2. Without direction or planning; haphazardly.

Example: If security forces sustain the pressure, the militants will be *willy-nilly* forced to the negotiating table.

Wishy-washy

Adj. 1. Weak or thin (drink or soup).

    2. Feeble or insipid.

Example: Shah Rukh Khan sometimes portray's *wishy-washy* characters on screen.

Eponyms or Name Words

Wittingly or unwittingly, some people (or places) have left their names for posterity through words that were coined after them. Called **eponyms**, these words tell interesting tales about their origins. Eponyms are derived from the names of real, fictional, mythical or spurious persons, places or characters, although many eponyms come from a person's surname.

Aphrodisiac
N. *Food, drink or drug that stimulates sexual desire.*
Aphrodite was the Greek goddess of love and beauty.

Armageddon
N. 1. *The last battle between good and evil before the Day of Judgement (as mentioned in the New Testament).*
   2. *A catastrophic conflict.*
The word is derived from the Hebrew, *Har Megiddon* or *Hill of Megiddo*. The word now means a *final, decisive conflict*.

****

Bayonet
N. *A long blade or dagger fixed to the muzzle of a rifle for use in hand-to-hand fighting.*
Bayonne, a town in south-west France, has been immortalised with the word *bayonet*, where these long daggers were first made.

Bloomers
N. 1. *Historical.* Women's loose-fitting trousers, gathered at the knee or ankle.
   2. Women's loose-fitting knee-length knickers.

In 1849, Mrs Elizabeth Smith Miller invented a working model of a garment and showed them to famous women's rights activist, Amelia Jenks *Bloomer*. The garment was both modest (they then reached down to the ankles) and convenient. Mrs Bloomer loved the garment and promptly sponsored it... and the word *bloomers* soon saw the light of day.

Bobbitt

V. *To forcibly cut off the male organ or penis.*

In the 1990s, an American housewife, Lorena *Bobbitt*, was fed up of her husband's never-ending affairs. When umpteen warnings failed to have the desired results, in a fit of anger one night, Lorena Bobbitt simply lopped off her husband's penis while he was sleeping.

Bowdlerize

V. *Remove from (a text) material that is regarded as improper, offensive or politically incorrect.*

In 1818, an English editor Dr Thomas *Bowdler* published an expurgated edition of *The Family Shakespeare*. In Bowdler's edition, "those words and expressions are omitted which cannot with propriety be read aloud in a family"!

Boycott

V. *With from commercial or social relations with, as a form of punishment or in protest, refuse to buy or handle goods for this reason.*
N. *An act of boycotting.*

The first person to be so boycotted in 1880 was Captain Charles C *Boycott*, an Irish land agent, whose tenants tried to get their rents reduced through this stratagem.

Bushism

N. *To indulge in malapropism while speaking; to utter a nonsensical word or sentence that conveys the opposite of what the person wishes to say.*

George W. *Bush*, the 43rd President of the United States, gets the credit for inadvertently being the creator of this word. Some popular Bushisms:

- ❏ "I firmly believe the death tax is good for people from all walks of life throughout our society."

- "I love the idea of a school in which people come to get educated and stay in the same state in which they're educated."

- "We are ready for any unforeseen event which may or may not happen."

- "To those of you who received honours, awards and distinctions, I say well done. And to the 'C' students, I say you, too, can be President of the US."

Analysts conjecture that President George Bush could either be suffering from **dyslexia** (*word-blindness*) or **aphasia** (*the inability to express thoughts in words*).

****

Calicut
N. 1. A type of plain white or unbleached cotton cloth.
   2. Printed cotton fabric.
The word is derived from *Calicut*, a seaport in south-west India, where the fabric originated.

Casanova
N. *A man notorious for seducing women and having many affairs.*
Italian adventurer and smooth talker Giovanni Giacomo *Casanova* (1725-98), was noted for his affairs across different nations. In his *Memoirs*, he gave lurid accounts of his many love affairs, claiming to have slept with well over one thousand women, some of his lovers being mothers and daughters.

Chauvinism
N. 1. *Aggressive or exaggerated patriotism.*
   2. *Excessive or prejudiced support or loyalty for one's own cause, group or sex.*
Nicolas *Chauvin*, said to have been a soldier in Napoleon's army, displayed such exaggerated loyalty and patriotism, even after the fall of Napoleon, that others ridiculed him.

Cicerone
N. *A guide who gives information to sightseers.*
A writer and the greatest orator of ancient Rome, Marcus Tullius *Cicero* (106-43 BC) was renowned for his eloquent speeches. Modern tourists

guides have to be eloquent speakers with a thorough knowledge of the historic locales they cover, hence the word *cicerone*.

****

Don Juan
N. *A seducer of women; a philanderer.*
The word comes from *Don Juan*, a legendary Spanish nobleman notorious for his dissolute life and philandering ways.

Draconian
Adj. (Of laws) *excessively harsh and severe.*
Athenian legislator *Draco* compiled the first written code of laws in ancient Athens. For almost all crimes, even petty ones, he assigned the death penalty. Soon, people began saying that his laws were written in blood, not ink, with a lot of justification.

Dumdum
N. *A kind of soft-nosed bullet that expands on impact and inflicts severe lacerations.*
Also termed **dumdum bullet**, the word comes from *Dum Dum*, the name of a town and ordinance depot near Kolkata, where these bullets were first made.

Dunce
N. *A person who is slow at learning.*
The word was originally an epithet for followers of the 13th century Scottish theologian John *Duns* Scotus, who was intelligent and learned! However, humanists ridiculed his followers as enemies of learning and deliberately referred to them as *Dunces*.

****

Epicure
N. *A person who takes special pleasure in fine food and drink.*
Greek philosopher *Epicurus* (341-270 BC) taught that pleasure, particularly mental pleasure, was the highest good.

Erotic
Adj. *Of, relating to, or tending to arouse sexual desire or excitement.*
Eros was the Greek god of love.

****

Fabian
Adj. *Employing a cautious, persistent but dilatory strategy to wear out an enemy while avoiding direct battle.*

Roman general Quintus *Fabius* Maximus was known for his delaying tactics in his war against Hannibal. After he was appointed dictator in 217 BC, he decided that it was better if the Roman army used cautious delaying tactics rather than engage Hannibal's army in pitched battles. He harassed Hannibal's army, cut off its supplies and repeatedly raided enemy lines. He soon came to be known as *Cunctator* or *Delayer*. Today, his policies are described as *Fabian*, denoting a gradual, step-by-step change.

Frangipani
N. *A tropical American tree or shrub with clusters of fragrant white, pink or yellow flowers; perfume obtained from this plant.*

The word is derived from Marquis Muzio *Frangipani*, a 16th century Italian nobleman who invented a perfume for scenting gloves.

Frankfurter
N. *Seasoned smoked sausage made of beef and pork.*

Originally from the German city of *Frankfurt*, they were referred to as *Frankfurter Wurst* or Frankfurt sausage.

****

Gerrymander
V. *Manipulate the boundaries of (an electoral constituency) to favour one's party or class.*

The term comes from Governor Elbridge *Gerry* of Massachusetts and the word *salamander*, due to the supposed similarity and the shape of a new voting district created when he was in office, which was supposed to favour his party.

Geronimo
Exclaim. *Used to express exhilaration when leaping or moving quickly.*

The word originated during the Second World War, when American paratroopers adopted it as a slogan, associating it with the Apache Indian chief Geronimo (1829?–1909).

Guppies

N. *A small freshwater fish native to tropical American and widely kept in aquaria, which bears live young.*

In 1868, Trinidadian clergyman RJ Lechmere *Guppy* sent the first specimen to the British Museum. The fish have since come to be known as *guppies*.

Gypsy

N. *A member of a travelling with dark skin and hair, who speak Romany (a language related to Hindi) and who traditionally live by itinerant trade and fortune telling.*

The people were originally known as *Gipcyan*, which was short for Egyptian, since the Gypsies were erroneously believed to have come from *Egypt*.

****

Hector

V. *Talk to someone in a bullying way.*

The term comes from the Trojan warrior *Hector* in Homer's *Iliad*. Originally, it denoted a hero but later came to mean a braggart or bully.

Hermaphrodite

N. *A person or animal having both male and female sexual organs or other sexual characteristics.* **Adj.** *Of or denoting a person, animal or plant of this kind.*

Greek legend has it that *Hermaphroditos* (the son of Hermes and Aphrodite) became joined in one body with the nymph Salmacis, hence the word *hermaphrodite*.

****

Iris

N. 1. *A flat, coloured, ring-shaped membrane behind the cornea of the eye, with an adjustable circular opening (the pupil) in the centre of the eye.*

  2. *A plant with showy flowers, typically purple or yellow and sword-shaped leaves.*

In Greek mythology, *Iris* was the goddess of the rainbow and messenger of the gods.

****

Jeremiad

N. *A long, mournful complaint or lamentation; list of woes.*

The word comes thanks to the *Lamentations of Jeremiah* in the *Old Testament*. Therefore, **Jeremiah** (**n.**) is *a person who complains continually or foretells disaster.*

Jodhpurs

Pl. N. *Trousers worn for horse riding that are close-fitting below the knee and have reinforced patches on the inside of the leg.*

No prizes for guessing where this word is derived from – the Indian city of *Jodhpur* in Rajasthan.

Juggernaut

N. 1. *Any relentless, overwhelming and destructive force.*

    2. *A large heavy vehicle, especially an articulated truck.*

The term is derived from Hindu god *Jagannath*, Lord of the World, an incarnation of Lord Vishnu, whose idol was hauled along on a large chariot, which so excited devotees that they would fling themselves before it and get crushed under its wheels.

Judas

N. *A person who betrays a friend, a traitor.*

Judas Iscariot was the disciple who betrayed Jesus Christ at the Last Supper.

****

Knickerbockers

N. *Full breeches gathered and banded just below the knee; knickers.*

Derived from Diedrich *Knickerbocker*, the fictitious author of *History of New York* (1809), which was actually authored by Washington Irving (1783–1859). The meaning is supposedly derived from the knee breeches worn by Dutch settlers in Irving's book.

****

Laconic

Adj. *Using very few words in speaking or communicating; terse.*

The word comes from the town of *Lakon* or *Laconia* in Spartan, the Spartans being known for their terse speech.

Leotard
N. *A close-fitting, stretchy one-piece garment covering the body to the top of the thighs, worn for dance, gymnastics and exercise.*
The name comes from the French trapeze artist, Jules *Leotard* (1842-70).

Levi's
N. *A trademark used for denim trousers.*
Bavarian immigrant to the US and a clothing merchant, *Levi* Strauss (1830-1902) ensured his place in the sun through his creation.

Lynch
V. *The killing of someone by a group for an alleged offence, without a legal trial, especially by hanging.*
Captain William *Lynch* (1742-1820), an American plantation owner and vigilante, was the head of a self-constituted judicial tribunal in Virginia (September 22, 1780) who indulged in such extra-judicial killings.

****

Macadam
N. *Broken stone used in compacted layers for surfacing roads and paths, typically bound with tar or bitumen.*
Named after the British surveyor John L. *McAdam*, macadamised roads are ones that we see often in India, but may not have not what they were called.

Mackintosh
N. *A full-length waterproof coat.*
We need to thank Scottish inventor Charles *Macintosh* (1766-1843) for the coat and the word. The coat was originally made by cementing layers of cloth with rubber.

Machiavellian
Adj. *Cunning, crafty, scheming and unscrupulous, especially in politics and business.*
In his work *The Prince* (1532), Italian statesman and writer Niccolo *Machiavelli* (1469-1527) says that the acquisition and use of power may necessitate the use of unethical means. A *Machiavellian* person will therefore seek to get what he desires by fair or foul means.

Martinet
N. *A strict disciplinarian, particularly in the armed forces.*
The 17th century French drillmaster General Jean *Martinet* was supposed to have been a stickler for discipline and has thereby left us a permanent legacy.

Masochism
N. *The tendency to derive pleasure, especially sexual gratification, from one's own pain or humiliation.*
Austrian novelist Leopold von Sacher-Masoch (1835-1895) described an abnormal mental condition in which the person derives pleasure from being physically and emotionally abused and punished by someone he loves.

Maverick
N. *An orthodox or independent-minded person.*
A Texas rancher of the 1840s, Samuel A *Maverick* refused to brand his cattle, unlike other ranchers. Initially, the word was only applied to unbranded cattle. Later, the term was applied to anybody who did not follow common rules.

McCoy
N. Informal. *The real thing; the genuine article.*
Used in the phrase, **the real McCoy**, there are two versions about its origins.

1. It may have come from an advertising slogan, *the real Mackay*, used by the whiskey distillers G. Mackay and Co.
2. It could have come from the name of the American inventor Elijah *McCoy*.

Mesmerise
V. *Capture the whole attention of; fascinate or transfix.*
Austrian physician Franz A *Mesmer* (1734-1815) created waves in Vienna and Paris when he claimed that there existed a power that could hold people in a trance, which he termed animal magnetism. Soon, people began referring to this power as *mesmerism*. Today, the term hypnotism is more popular.

****

Narcissism
N. *Excessive or erotic interest in oneself and one's physical appearance.*
Narcissus was a handsome youth in Greek mythology who fell in love with his own reflection in a pool.

Nemesis
N. 1. *Just punishment or retribution.*
    2. *Anyone or anything that seems to be the inevitable cause of someone's downfall or defeat.*
In Greek mythology, *Nemesis* was the goddess of divine punishment or retributive justice.

Nicotine
N. *A colourless poisonous alkaloid derived from the tobacco plant and used as an insecticide. It is the substance in tobacco to which smokers can become addicted.*
Four centuries ago, French diplomat Jean *Nicot* (1530-1600) bought some tobacco seeds from a Flemish trader. Nicot's efforts to popularise the plant in Europe have ensured he has entered the dictionary.

****

Oedipus complex
N. *According to Freudian theory, the complex of emotions aroused in a young child by an unconscious sexual desire for the parent of the opposite sex.*
Oedipus was a character in Greek mythology who unwittingly killed his father and married his mother.

Onanism
N. 1. *Masturbation.*
    2. *Coitus interruptus.*
After *Onan*, son of Judah (*Genesis* 38:9), who is said to have practised *coitus interruptus*.

****

Pandora's box
N. *A process that generates many complicated problems, once it is begun.*

Greek mythology tells us that *Pandora* (the first woman) was sent to the earth with a jar or box of evils and was explicitly warned against opening it. Unable to contain her curiosity, she opened the box and let out all the evils, which have since been plaguing the earth; hope alone remained in the box.

Panic
N. *Sudden uncontrollable fear or anxiety, (informal) frenzied hurry to do something.*
Derived from Greek god *Pan*, renowned for causing terror.

Pyrrhic victory
Adj. *A victory won at too great a cost to be worthwhile for the victor.*
Pyrrhus, King of Epirus, defeated the Romans at Asculum in 279 BC but sustained such heavy losses that he is said to have exclaimed: "Another such victory and we are undone."

Pasteurise
V. *Subject milk, wine etc to a process of partial sterilisation, especially by heating.*
Derived from French chemist and bacteriologist, Louis *Pasteur* (1822-95), who devised the process to prevent the spoilage of milk and other liquids.

Platonic
Adj. 1. *Of or associated with the Greek philosopher Plato or his ideas.*
2. *Of love or friendship that is intimate and affectionate without being sexual.*

The word comes to us from *Plato* (427-347 BC).

****

Quisling
N. *A traitor who collaborates with an occupying enemy force.*
During the Second World War, Major Vidkun *Quisling* ruled Norway on behalf of the German occupying forces. His name is notorious ever since.

Quixotic
Adj. *Impractically idealistic or fanciful.*

The word comes from the eccentric hero Don *Quixote*, hero of Miguel Cervantes novel by the same name.

****

Rabelaisian

N. *An admirer of French satirist Francois Rabelais (1494?-1553).* **Adj.** *Of or like Rabelais or his writing; marked by exuberant imagination and coarse or earthy humour.*

Francois *Rabelais* was a French humanist and writer of satirical attacks on medieval scholasticism and superstition, the most notable of these works being *Pantagruel* and (1532) and *Gargantua* (1534).

Ritzy

Adj. (Informal) *expensively stylish.*

From Swiss hotelier Cesar *Ritz* (1850-1918), who opened luxury hotels.

****

Sadism

N. *The tendency to derive sexual gratification or general pleasure from inflicting pain, suffering or humiliation on others.*

Frenchman Marquis de *Sade* (1740-1814) took great delight in torturing his friends and mistresses. In his writings, he described the pleasure a person derived in tormenting someone he loved. These morbid, abnormally cruel tendencies shocked the nation. Today, a *sadistic* person is anyone who indulges in this kind of behaviour.

Incidentally, a **masochist** is a person who derives sexual pleasure or gratification from tormenting his own self or being tormented and humiliated by others. And a **sadomasochist** is a person who displays both sadistic and masochistic tendencies.

Sandwich

N. *Two pieces of bread with a filling of food between them.*

John Montagu, fourth Earl of *Sandwich* (1718-92) and an English diplomat, supposedly rustled up a quick meal in this way.

Sanforised

Adj. Trademark. (Of cotton or other fabric) pre-shrunk by a controlled compressive process.

The word originated in the 1930s from the name of the American inventor, *Sanford L Cluett*.

Saturday

N. *The day of the week that falls before Sunday and after Friday.*

The term for this day of the week comes from *Saturn*, the Roman god of agriculture.

Sidhuism

N. *Witty speech peppered with uncommon phrases; repartee; the gift of the gab.*

Derived from ex-Indian opening batsman, Navjot Singh *Sidhu*, who is making more waves as an eloquent and witty cricket commentator than he ever did as India's opening batsman. Some Sidhuisms of 2004:

   1. *The room for improvement is the biggest room in the world.*

   2. *The future is a haze and the past is a bucketful of ashes.*

Spartan

N. *Of or relating to Sparta (a city-state in ancient Greece) or its people.*

Adj. **1.** *Rigorously self-disciplined or self-restrained.*

   2. *Simple, frugal or austere.*

   3. *Marked by brevity of speech, terse.*

The Spartan's were known for their legendary brevity. When Philip of Macedonia (Alexander the Great's father) was on the borders of *Sparta*, legend has it that he sent a terse message: "Friend or foe?" The message asked whether the Spartan's wished to see him as a friend or foe. Living up to their legendary reputation for brevity, the Spartans sent a one-word reply: "Neither."

Spoonerism

N. *An error in speech in which the initial letters or sounds of two or more words are accidentally transposed, with humorous results.*

The English scholar, Reverend William Archibald (1844-1930) Spooner for this habit of his, which may have been embarrassing for him, but seemed hilarious to listeners. For instance, *You have hissed the mystery lectures* instead of *You have missed the history lectures*.

****

Tantalise

V. *Torment or tease with the sight or promise of something that is unobtainable, withheld or out of reach.*

Greek mythology tells us that *Tantalus*, the mythical King of Phrygia, was punished for his crimes by being provided with fruit and water that receded when he reached for them.

Teddy bear

N. *A soft toy bear.*

US President *Theodore* Roosevelt (1858-1919) was an enthusiastic bear-hunter, affectionately known as *Teddy*. Somehow, the name of this avid bear-hunter stuck as an appellation for the toy bear!

Thursday

N. *The day of the week before Friday and after Wednesday.*

For this day of the week, we need to thank *Thor*, the Norse god of thunder, who gave us Thor's day.

Tuesday

N. *The day before Wednesday and after Monday.*

Tiw was the Germanic god of war and the sky.

****

Utopia

N. *An imaginary perfect place or state.*

Utopia was the title of a book (1516) by Sir Thomas More. The word was coined from the Greek *ou* (not) and *topos* (place). *Utopian* denotes an *idealistic state* or an *idealistic reformer*.

Uzi

N. *A type of sub-machine gun.*

The term originated in the 1950s from *Uziel* Gal (1923-2002), the Israeli army officer who designed this weapon.

****

Valentine

N. *A card sent (often anonymously) on St Valentine's Day (February 14) to a person one loves or is attracted to; a person to whom one sends such a card.*

After Saint *Valentine*, a third century Christian martyr.

Vandal

N. *A person who deliberately destroys or damages public or private property.*

The *Vandals* were a Germanic people who ravaged Gaul, Spain, Rome and North Africa in the 4th and 5th centuries.

Venereal

Adj. 1. *Of or relating to venereal disease.*
2. *(Formal) of or relating to sexual desire or sexual intercourse.*
Venereal is derived from *Venus*, the Roman goddess of love.

****

Wednesday

N. *The day of the week before Thursday and after Tuesday.*

Named after the Germanic god *Odin* or *Woden*, the god of wisdom, culture and war.

Winchester

N. 1. (Also **Winchester rifle**) Trademark, *a breech-loading, side-action repeating rifle.*
2. (Also **Winchester disk** or **drive**) Computing, *a disk drive in a sealed unit containing a high-capacity hard disk and the read-write heads.*

The rifle was named after the American rifle manufacturer Oliver F *Winchester* (1866-1974). The computer disk drive acquired the name because its original numerical designation corresponded to the calibre of the rifle.

****

Xanadu

N. *An imaginary wonderful place.*

The word is an alteration of *Shang-tu*, an ancient city in south-east Mongolia, as portrayed in Coleridge's poem, *Kubla Khan* (1816).

Xerox

N. Trademark. *A xerographic copying process; a copy made using such a process.* **V.** *Copy (a document) by such a process.*

The term arose in the 1950s, based on *xerography*, which was derived from the company's name *Xerox*. Years ago, Xerox protested that the trademark name of the company could not be used as a verb and splashed ads to drive the point home. Despite this, a photocopy is today termed a *xerox*, even if erroneously.

****

Yale

N. Trademark. *A type of lock with a latch bolt and a flat key with a serrated edge.*
Named after the American locksmith Linus *Yale* Jr (1821-68).

****

Zany

Adj. *Amusingly unconventional and idiosyncratic.* **N.** *A zany person.*
From *Zanni*, Venetian form of *Gianni* (John), the stock name of servants acting as clowns in the commedia dell'arte.

Zoroastrianism

N. *A monotheistic pre-Islamic religion of ancient Persia founded by the prophet Zoroaster (Zarathustra) in the 7th century BC.*
The Parsis of India are followers of the Persian prophet *Zoroaster* (660-583).

∞

The Magic of Newborn Words

This chapter is devoted to neologisms – *a newly coined word or expression*. When words are first coined, instant approval is not what they meet with. Usually the first reaction is instant disapproval! For instance, when President John Fitzgerald Kennedy first used the word *finalized*, much to the horror of purists and most other users, the usage was roundly condemned. Today, we take the word for granted.

Some of the words presented in this chapter are currently in colloquial and/or Internet usage and may not be found even in the latest dictionaries. Wait a few years, though, and they will gatecrash into every respectable dictionary.

Andropause (or Viropause)
The term refers to the end of virility (created from a combination of androgen/virility and menopause). If *women* have *men*opause, obviously men had to have something other than *men*opause. The prefix *andro* refers to something *male* or *mascusline* (from the Greek *andr*), hence *andropause*.

Artsy
Pretending to be artistic, overly artistic.

****

Blog
This is a web page consisting of frequently updated, chronological entries on a particular topic. It is a form of free publishing that is typically updated daily.

****

Criminal menopause
This refers to a stage in life during which an older, habitual criminal loses interest in crime, or when an older prisoner no longer poses any threat to society.

Cyborg
This is a human being who has certain physiological processes and physical abilities that are aided or controlled by mechanical or electronic devices that are embedded into the body. Once purely science fiction, the first cyborg became a reality in 2003.

Cybernetics
This is the science of communications and automatic control systems in machines as well as in living beings.

****

Flash mob
The word refers to a large group of people who gather in a usually predetermined location, perform some brief action and then quickly disperse.

Floortime
This is a therapeutic or parenting technique wherein an adult engages in creative play with a child that often includes getting down on the floor with the child.

419 scam
The four-one-nine scam is a fraud, particularly one originating in Nigeria, in which a person is asked for money to help secure the release of, and so earn a percentage of, a much larger sum.

Also referred to as **419 fraud**, **419 scheme** or **419 con**, the classic **419 scam** asks the victim to help some hapless relative of a deposed dictator remove millions of dollars out of the conman's country. The conman (or woman!) offers the victim a percentage of this fictitious pot of gold, hoping to suck the victim into paying all sorts of fees to get trunks of money out of Nigeria, Sierra Leone, the Philippines or whatever exotic country the conman chooses. Ultimately, the money is never sent, but the victims are often duped to the tune of thousands of dollars.

****

Googol
A cardinal number that's equivalent to ten raised to the power of a hundred. The word was purportedly coined in the 1940s by the young nephew of American mathematician, Edward Kasner.

****

Hathos
These refer to feelings of pleasure derived from hating someone or something. The word is obviously a take-off from **pathos**: a quality or characteristic that evokes pity or sadness.

****

Kippers
An acronym (*kids in parents' pockets eroding retirement savings*), it refers to an adult son or daughter, particularly one over 30 years or more, who still lives with his or her parents.

****

Location awareness
This is the capability to detect the exact or relative location of a device, particularly a wireless device such as a cell phone.

****

Passive overeating
The term refers to excessive eating of foods that are high in fat because the human body is slow to recognise the caloric content of rich foods; also, eating whatever is put before you, even to the point of discomfort.

****

Quiet party
This is a party in which talking and other loud noises are prohibited and where guests communicate using handwritten notes. These unconventional parties ensure that singles do not have to bother about trying to sustain any sort of conversation in the midst of overpowering background music or noise. Participants pay a minimal fee to enter. They are then given envelopes, paper and pencils and allowed only to "whisper" in areas designated for low-volume

conversations. After a few minutes of drinks, whispers and giggles, the bits of paper start flying.

****

Sex grab

Modern-day overcrowding in cities seems to have lead to this condition and the coining of a new term: *sex grab*. It refers to a passer-by (usually a male) reaching out for or actually touching the genitals or breasts of a pedestrian (naturally, a female).

This condition is particularly encountered in overcrowded local trains in cities like Mumbai and in jam-packed buses of Delhi, Mumbai and other metro cities.

School refusal

The condition refers to an extreme fear of attending school. The condition is particularly fond amongst children who stammer or have some other impediment.

Child psychologists in the West use **school refusal** as a medical term. A child displaying this condition might pretend to be sick or prefer to stay home because of a feeling of safety and security. Some children will refuse to get out of bed or waste as much time as possible while getting ready in the morning. Others will use any excuse to throw a tantrum and avoid going to school. Some children will even experience physical symptoms like stomachache, headache or nausea.

Shouting head

A loud and aggressive person, particularly one who is a television pundit or commentator, is termed a **shouting head**. In India, Manoj Raghuvanshi is known to hector secular guests who belong to the other side of the saffron divide.

Social networking

This refers to the use of a Web site to connect with people who share similar personal or professional interests, particularly where the people in the site's database are connected to each other as friends, friends of friends, and so on.

Spam

These are irrelevant or inappropriate messages sent via the Internet to a large number of users or newsgroups.

The word originated in the 1930s from **sp**iced h**am**. The Internet meaning is supposedly derived from a sketch (set in a café) by the British comedy group Monty Python where every item on the menu includes spam.

Spim

This refers to unsolicited commercial messages sent via an instant messaging system.

There is no system that marketers will not exploit – and instant messaging is the latest system that has now caught their fancy. Spam is something that we are already familiar with (explained in the previous paragraphs). Add Instant Messaging or IM to spam and voila! – you have spim.

Stink lines

In an illustration or cartoon, you will notice wavy lines that appear over an object to indicate that it smells bad – so **stink lines** indicate the metaphorical stench emanating from something that is extremely bad.

****

Terror management

This indicates a set of personal or cultural practices or beliefs that enable an individual or a society to ignore or accept the inevitability of death. Also referred to as: **terror management theory**.

****

White food

Processed foods like white sugar and all-purpose flour, or starchy foods such as potatoes, rice and pasta are referred to as **white food**.

Word burst

This refers to a rapid rise in both the frequency with which a word is used in a particular context and the rate at which the word's usage increases over time.

∞

The Portmanteau Combos

A portmanteau word is one that blends the sounds and combines the meanings of two others. The word is derived from the French *portmanteau*, combined from *porter* ('to carry') plus *manteau* ('mantle'). While the word *portmanteau* originated in the 16th century, Lewis Carroll is credited with coining the term *portmanteau word* (in *Through the Looking Glass*) based on the fact that a *portmanteau bag* is one that opens into two equal parts.

However, some portmanteau words catch on and latch on to the lexicon; others don't and simply fade away into silent sunsets, having enjoyed their 15 minutes of glory. Here is a list of portmanteau words that readers could write in and add on to as and when they come across ones not mentioned here. The meanings of all such words are apparent from the combination. Most of these words will not be found in standard dictionaries or even the enlarged editions. But readers can exercise their grey cells in putting two and two together to deduce the meaning of these words.

01. Adflation (advertising + inflation)
02. Beautility (beauty + utility)
03. Bit (binary + digit)
04. Bitini (bitsy + bikini)
05. Bonk (bang + conk)
06. Brunch (breakfast + lunch)
07. Camcorder (camera + recorder)
08. Chortle (chuckle + snort)
09. Cremains (cremated + remains)
10. Chunnel (channel + tunnel)

11. Diplonomics (diplomacy + economics)
12. E-commerce (electronic + commerce)
13. Email (electronic + mail)
14. Faction (fact + fiction)
15. Fantabulous (fantastic + fabulous)
16. Fanzine (fanatic + magazine)
17. Feminar (feminine + seminar)
18. Frarority (fraternity + sorority)
19. Gasohol (gasoline + alcohol)
20. Ginormous (gigantic + enormous)
21. Guestimate (guess + estimate)
22. Hi-tech (high + technology)
23. Heliport (helicopter + airport)
24. Internet (international + network)
25. Interpol (international + police)
26. Jackpot (jack + pot)
27. Jaywalk (Jay + walk)
28. Jerkwater (jerk + water)
29. Joypad (joystick + pad)
30. Laundromat (laundry + automat)
31. Manimal (man + animal)
32. Medevac (medical + evacuation)
33. Medicare (medical + care)
34. Mobike (motor + bike)
35. Motel (motor + hotel)
36. Motorcade (motorcar + cavalcade)
37. Newscast (news + broadcast)
38. Oxbridge (Oxford + Cambridge)
39. Paratroops (parachute + troops)
40. Sci-fi (science + fiction)
41. Sexploitation (sexual + exploitation)
42. Shamateur (sham + amateur)
43. Smog (smoke + fag)
44. Splurge (splash + surge)
45. Telecast (television + broadcast)

46. Telecon (telephone + conversation)
47. Televangelist (television + evangelist)
48. Transistor (transfer + resistor)
49. Vash (volcanic + ash)
50. Workfar (work + welfare)

Talking Numbers

Numbers have always fascinated mankind. The ancients attached mystical significance to numbers and believed they held all the mysterious to the origins and systematic functioning of the universe.

Indeed, numbers can talk if only we know how to decipher their secret meanings. The word *number* itself has many meanings, besides the regular mathematical definition, one of these being: *a song, dance or other musical item*, according to the *Concise Oxford English Dictionary*.

In this chapter, we will let numbers do the talking in unlocking the meaning of hitherto esoteric or meaningless words. The words on these pages are either directly derived from numbers or have numbers embedded in their etymology (roots) or meanings.

Abacus

N. *A frame with rows of wires, along which beads (in descending numbers) are slid, used for calculating.*

One of the opening words in any dictionary, the abacus can be considered the primitive forefather of modern calculators and the computer. Today, the abacus with its colourful beads is primarily used to teach little children how to count.

****

Baker's dozen

Phrase. *A group of thirteen.*

In the days of yore, a baker's dozen consisted of 13, instead of 12. Bakers adopted the custom of adding an extra loaf to a dozen sold to the retailer, as the thirteenth was the latter's profit! Bakers were also said to follow this practice to ensure the proper weight and avoid any penalty for short measure.

Biannual
Adj. *Occurring twice a year; semi-annual.*

Biennial
Adj. *Taking place every two years; lasting for two years.*

Bicameral
Adj. *With two chambers* (as in a legislative body).

Bicentenary
N. *The two-hundredth anniversary of a significant event.*

Bifurcate
V. *Divide into two branches or forks.*

Bigamy
N. *The offence of marrying someone while already being married to another person.*
Monogamy, on the other hand, is *the practice of being married to or having a sexual relationship with only one person at a time.*

Bilingual
Adj. *Speaking two languages fluently.*

Bisexual
Adj. 1. *Sexually attracted to both men and women.*
   2. *Having characteristics of both sexes.*
N. *A person who is sexually attracted to both men and women.*

****

Cabal
N. 1. *A secret political clique or faction.*
   2. *A committee of five ministers under King Charles II, whose surnames happened to begin with C, A, B, A and L.*

Caucus
N. 1. *A meeting of members of a legislative body, who belong to a particular political party, to select candidates or decide policy.*
   2. *A group of people with shared concerns within a larger organisation.*

Centenarian
N. *A person who is a hundred or more years old.*

Centenary
N. *The hundredth anniversary of a significant event.*

Clique
N. *A small group of people who spend time together and do not readily allow others to join them.*

Cipher
N. 1. *A code or a key to a code.*
   2. *Zero* (rarely used).
   3. *An unimportant person or thing.*

From the first meaning, the word **decipher** is derived, implying: *to convert from code into normal language or succeed in understanding or interpreting something obscure or unclear.*

Coterie
N. *A small exclusive group of people who share similar interests or tastes.*

Couplet
N. *A pair of successive lines of verse, usually rhyming and of the same length.*

****

Debut
N. *A person's first appearance in a capacity or role.*

Decade
N. 1. *A period of ten years.*
   2. *A set or group of ten.*

Decathlon
N. *An athletic event in which each competitor takes part in the same ten events.*

Decimate
V. 1. *Kill or destroy a large proportion of; drastically reduce the strength of.*
   2. *(In ancient Rome) kill one in every ten (of a group of soldiers) as a punishment for the mutiny of the whole group.*

Dichotomy

N. 1. *A division or contrast between two things that are opposed or entirely different.*

2. (Botany) *repeated branching into two equal parts.*

Dilemma

N. 1. *A situation in which a difficult choice has to be made between two or more alternatives.*

2. (Logic) *an argument forcing an opponent to choose either of two unfavourable alternatives.*

Doublespeak

N. *Deliberately ambiguous or obscure language.*

Novelist George Orwell coined the word in 1949.

Double standard

N. *A rule or principle applied unfairly in different ways to different people.*

Double take

N. *A delayed reaction to something unexpected, immediately after one's first reaction.*

Double whammy

N. (Informal) *a twofold blow or setback.*

Duo

N. *A pair of people or things, especially in music or entertainment.*

Duologue

N. *A play or part of a play with speaking roles for two actors only.*

Duplicitous

Adj. 1. *Deceitful.*

2. Law (of a charge or plea) *containing more than one allegation.*

****

Enumerate

V. 1. *Mention one by one.*

2. *Establish the number of.*

Equivocal
Adj. *Unclear in meaning or intention; ambiguous.*

****

Fathom
N. 1. *A unit of length equal to six feet (1.8 metres) that's primarily used with reference to the depth of water.*

V. 2. *Understand something after much thought* (usually used with a negative).

Fifth columnist
N. *A person within a country or organisation who works for the enemy.*

****

Gaggle
N. 1. *A flock of geese.*
   2. (Informal) *a disorderly group of people.*

Googol
Cardinal number. *Equivalent to ten raised to the power of a hundred.*

****

Heterosexual
Adj. *Sexually attracted to the opposite sex.*

Homosexual
Adj. *Feeling or involving sexual attraction to the people of one's own sex.*

The term for a homosexual woman is **lesbian**. A homosexual man is informally termed a **homo**.

****

Iota
N. *An extremely small amount* (usually used with a negative).
Example: There was no *iota* of doubt that OJ Simpson had murdered his wife.

****

Legion

N. 1. *A division of 3,000–6,000 in the ancient Roman army.*
   2. *A vast number of people or things.*
Adj. *Great in number.*
Example: Amitabh Bachchan's fans are *legion*.

****

Monogram

N. *A motif of two or more interwoven letters, typically a person's initials.*
V. *Decorate with a monogram.*

Monologue

N. 1. *A long speech by one actor in a play or film.*
   2. *A long, tedious speech by one person during a conversation.*

Monopoly

N. 1. *The exclusive possession or control of the supply of or trade in a commodity or service.*
   2. *Exclusive possession or control of something.*

Monotheism

N. *The doctrine or belief that there is only one God.*

Myriad

N. *An indefinitely great number.*
Adj. *Innumerable.*

****

Nonagenarian

N. *A person who is between 90 and 99 years.*

Numero uno

N. (Informal) *the best or most important person or thing.*

Numismatology

N. *Numismatics – the study or collection of coins, banknotes and medals.*

****

Octogenarian

N. *A person between 80 and 89 years.*

Oligarchy
N. *A small group of persons having control of a state; a state governed by such a group.*

One-track mind
N. *(Informal) a person preoccupied with one subject only, especially sex.*

One-trick pony
N. *A person or thing with only one special feature, talent or area of expertise.*

One-upmanship
N. *(Informal) the technique of gaining an advantage or feeling of superiority over another.*

****

Pentagon
N. 1. *A plane figure with five straight sides and five angles.*
    2. (The Pentagon) the headquarters of the US Department of Defence, near Washington DC.

Pentathlon
N. *An athletic event comprising five different events for each competitor, in particular* (also termed **modern pentathlon**) *a men's event involving fencing, shooting, swimming, riding and cross-country running.*

****

Quadrennial
Adj. *Lasting for or occurring every four years.*

Quarantine
N. *A state, period or place of isolation for people or animals that have arrived from elsewhere or been exposed to contagious disease.*
V. *Put in quarantine.*
The word is derived from Italian, *quarantina*, meaning *forty days*.

Quartet
N. 1. *A group of four people playing music or singing together.*
    2. *A set of four people or things.*

Quatrain
N. *A stanza of four lines, typically with alternate rhymes.*

Quinquegenarian
N. *A person between 50 and 59 years.*

Quinquennium
N. *A period of five years.*

Quintessence
N. 1. *The most perfect or typical example.*
   2. *A refined essence or extract of a substance.*

Quintet
N. 1. *A group of five people playing music or singing together.*
   2. *A set of five people or things.*

Quintuplet
N. *Each of five children born at one birth or delivery.*

Quorum
N. *The minimum number of members of an assembly or society that must be present at a meeting to make the proceedings valid.*

****

Raffle
N. *A lottery with goods as prizes.*
V. *Offer as a prize in a raffle.*

****

Schism
N. *A division between strongly opposed parties, caused by differences in opinions or belief.*

Schizophrenia
N. *A long-term mental disorder of a type involving a breakdown in the relation between thought, emotion and behaviour, leading to faulty perception, inappropriate actions and feelings and withdrawal from reality into fantasy and delusion.*

Second-degree
Adj. 1. (Medical) *denoting burns that cause blisters but not permanent scars.*
    2. (Law) *denoting a category of crime, especially murder, that is less serious than a first-degree crime.*

Second nature
N. *A tendency or habit that has become instinctive.*

Second-rate
Adj. *Of mediocre or inferior quality.*

Second string
N. *An alternative resource or course of action in case the first one fails.*

Second wind
N. *Regained ability to breathe freely during exercise, after having been out of breath.*

Septennial
Adj. *Lasting for or occurring every seven years.*

Septuagenarian
N. *A person between 70 and 79 years.*

Septuplet
N. *Each of seven children born at one birth.*

Sesquicentenary
N. *The one-hundredth-and-fiftieth anniversary of a significant event.*

Sexagenarian
N. *A person between 60 and 69 years.*

Sexcentenary
N. *The six-hundredth anniversary of a significant event.*

Sexennial
Adj. *Lasting for or recurring every six years.*

Sextet
N. 1. *A group of six people playing music or singing together.*
    2. *A set of six people or things.*

Sextuplets
N. *Each of six children born at one birth.*

Sixth sense
N. *A supposed intuitive faculty giving awareness not explicable in terms of normal perception.*

Sixty-nine
N. (Informal) *sexual activity between two people involving mutual oral stimulation of the genitals.*
The word is derived from the position of the couple that mimics the number 69.

****

Tercentenary
N. *A three-hundredth anniversary.*

Tertiary
Adj. 1. *Third in order or level, denoting education at a level beyond that provided by schools.*
    2. *Relating to or denoting medical treatment provided at a specialist institution.*

Third-degree
Adj. 1. (Medical) *denoting burns of the most severe kind.*
    2. (Law) *denoting the least serious category of crime, especially murder.*

N. (**The third degree**) *long and harsh questioning to obtain information or a confession.*

Third-rate
Adj. *Of inferior or very poor quality.*

Tithe
N. *One-tenth of annual produce or earnings, formerly taken as a tax for the support of the Church and clergy.*
V. *Subject to or pay as a tithe.*

Triad
N. *A group or set of three connected people or things.*

Trimester
N. 1. *A period of three months, especially as a division of the duration of pregnancy.*
   2. *Each of the three terms in an academic year.*

Trio
N. *A set or group of three.*

Tripe
N. 1. *The first or second stomach of a cow or other ruminant used as food.*
   2. (Informal) *nonsense; rubbish.*

Trisexual
Adj. *Sexually attracted to men, women and eunuchs.*
N. *A person who is sexually attracted to men, women and eunuchs.*
The word is not found in most dictionaries, since very few people discuss the condition or ever admit to being trisexuals! But readers will come across it in girlie magazines, although rarely.

Triskaidekaphobia
N. *Extreme superstition or fear regarding the number thirteen.*

Triumvirate
N. *A group of three powerful or notable people or things;* (in ancient Rome) *a group of three men holding power.*

Trivial
Adj. *Of little value or importance.*

Troika
N. 1. *A Russian vehicle pulled by a team of three horses.*
   2. *A group of three people working together, especially as administrators or managers.*

24-7
Adv. (Informal) *twenty-four hours a day, seven days a week; all the time.*

20/20
Adj. *Denoting vision of normal acuity.*

Two-bit
Adj. *Insignificant, cheap or worthless.*

Two-time
V. (Informal) *be unfaithful to* (a lover or spouse).

****

Unilateral
Adj. 1. *Performed by or affecting only one person or group.*
   2. *Relating to or affecting only one side of an organ, the body, etc.*

Unanimous
Adj. 1. *Fully in agreement.*
   2. *(Of an opinion, decision or vote) held or carried by everyone involved.*

****

Vacant possession
N. *Ownership of a property on completion of a sale, any previous occupant having moved out.*

****

Whit
N. *A very small amount.*

****

Yearling
N. *An animal that is a year old, or in its second year.*
Adj. *Having lived or existed for a year.*

Yesteryear
N. Poetic or literary. *Belonging to last year or the recent past.*

****

Zero hour
N. 1. *The time at which a military or any other operation is set to begin.*
   2. *Any crucial moment.*
   3. *Question hour in the Indian Parliament.*

Zilch
Pron. *Nothing; zero.*

∞

Commonly Confused Words

There are many words that sound like one another or have a somewhat similar meaning but may mean just the opposite, or have a meaning that has a subtle difference. It is imperative to know the right meaning of all the words you use. Here, we list the words where readers are apt to confuse one with the other. Once you learn the subtle or not-so-subtle difference in meaning, it is preferable to use the right word in the right context.

****

A – An
A is the first letter in the alphabet; used when mentioning someone or something for the first time; the indefinite article; used before a word with a consonant sound (for instance, a man; a tiger).

Example: A man can do a lot if he has the inclination.

An is the form of the indefinite article used before words that begin with a vowel sound, for instance, a hunter. However, when referring to the word 'hour', it will be *an* hour, simply because the 'h' in 'hour' is silent (i.e., not pronounced).

Example: It was *an* honour to be seated next to the chief guest.

Abjure – Adjure
Abjure refers to the *solemn renouncement* (of a belief or claim).

Example: The militants have promised to *abjure* violent means in their struggle.

Adjure is to *solemnly urge* (someone) *to do something*.

Example: The Prime Minister *adjured* the militants to give up their misguided struggle.

Accept – Except

Accept has multiple meanings:
1. *Consent to receive something that is offered.*
2. *Regard favourably or with approval.*
3. *Believe something to be valid or correct.*
4. *Take on a responsibility or liability etc.*

Example: The company will never *accept* any unfair demands of the union.

Except means *not included, other than, excluding.*

Example: *Except* for fair demands of the union, the company will reject all the others.

Adapt – Adopt

Adapt denotes *an adjustment to new conditions; making suitable for a new use or purpose.*

Example: All family members have to *adapt* to the situation when another child comes into its fold.

Adopt means
1. *Legally accept another's child and bring it up as one's own.*
2. *Choose to take up or follow (an option or a course of action).*

Example: Parents must *adopt* a measured approach with *adopted* children.

Adverse – Averse

Adverse denotes something *opposed or in opposition to, harmful or unfavourable* (circumstances etc.).

Example: Foreign troops are facing an *adverse* situation in Iraq.

Averse means *to have a feeling of opposition, distaste or aversion, to be strongly disinclined to.*

Example: Indian troops will be *averse* to a posting in Iraq.

Advice – Advise

Advice refers to *guidance or recommendation offered with regard to some future action.*

Example: Never give anyone unwanted *advice*.

Advise means *to recommend a course of action; offer advice to; inform someone about a fact or situation.*

Example: I was *advised* never to give unsolicited advice.

Affect – Effect

Affect means *make a difference to* or *touch the feelings of.*

Example: Your bad behaviour will *affect* our relations.

Effect denotes *a change that is a result or consequence of an action or other cause; bring about* (a change or result).

Example: Your bad behaviour will *effect* a major change in our relations.

Affluent – Effluent

Affluent denotes a *wealthy person.*

Example: Manisha Koirala hails from an affluent Nepali family.

Effluent means liquid waste or sewage discharged into a river or sea.

Example: Many companies were illegally discharging their *effluents* into the Yamuna River.

Aid – Aide

Aid denotes *help or support, material help given to a country that needs it.*

Example: The World Bank gives *aid* to many needy countries.

Aide means *an assistant to a political leader (or other important person).* The word is a short form of *aide-de-camp.*

Example: The Prime Minister has many *aides* to assist him in his daily tasks.

Allude – Elude

Allude means *hint at or refer to in passing* (usually *allude to*).

Example: The witness tried to *allude to* the fact that there was another motive for the murder.

Elude denotes *to evade or escape from (being caught or captured), to baffle.*

Example: The motive for this murder still seems to *elude* the police.

Allusion – Illusion

Allusion means *to hint or make indirect or implicit references to something.*

Example: There were *allusions* that the politician's promises were just a poll gimmick.

Illusion denotes *a false or unreal perception or impression.*

Example: Don't be under the *illusion* that the politician will fulfil any of his promises once he wins.

Altar – Alter

Altar refers to *a table or flat-topped block used for religious rituals, particularly in a Christian church.*

Example: The priest stands before the *altar* during mass.

Alter means *to change in character, appearance, direction etc.*

Example: You will have to *alter* your clothes since you have lost weight.

Amend – Emend

Amend means to *make changes or improvements to* (a text, document, proposal etc.)

Example: This Bill will only become law if the minister agrees to *amend* it.

Emend denotes to *correct and revise* (a text etc.)

Example: The Bill seems fine overall and may be passed, but the minister will only need to *emend* it.

Among – Between

Among means *situated more or less centrally in relation to several people; occurring or practised by some members of a group; indicating a division, choice or differentiation involving three or more participants.*

Example: There was no dispute *among* the brothers and sisters for the property.

Between means *at, into or across the space separating two objects, places or points; in the period separating two points in time; indicating a connection or relationship concerned with two or more parties.*

Example: There was a dispute *between* the two brothers over division of the property.

****

Bare – Bear
Bare means *a body or person that is not covered or clothed; to uncover or expose a part of the body; without elaboration; basic.*

Example: It is not in good taste for a man to expose his *bare* chest.

Bear denotes *to carry; to support; manage to tolerate; give birth to or to produce.*

Example: It is difficult to *bear* so much suffering in one's lifetime.

Beside – Besides
Beside means *alongside, at the side of* or *next to* (someone or something).

Example: At the parade, the foreign dignitary stood *beside* the Prime Minister.

Besides denotes *in addition to, apart from.*

Example: Besides the Prime Minister and the foreign dignitary, many other ministers were also present at the parade.

Biannual – Biennial
Biannual means *occurring twice a year.*

Example: The school exams are held on a *biannual* basis.

Biennial denotes *taking place every other year* or *once every two years.*

Example: The refresher course for teachers is held on a *biennial* basis.

Breath – Breathe
Breath means *air taken into or expelled from the lungs.*

Example: The doctor asked the patient to take a deep *breath*.

Breathe denotes *the physiological process of repeatedly taking air into the lungs and expelling it.*

Example: The doctor asked the patient to *breathe* deeply.

****

Can – May

Can means *to be able to (do something)*.

Example: A person can do a lot in life, if s/he wishes to.

May denotes *expressing the possibility or expressing a wish or hope*.

Example: A person may be able to do a lot in life if s/he puts in extra effort.

Carton – Cartoon

Carton is *a light cardboard container*.

Example: Pack the goods in cartons.

Cartoon denotes *a drawing made in an exaggerated style for humorous or satirical effect; a film made from a sequence of such images*.

Example: Two of the world's most loved cartoons are Laurel and Hardy and Tom and Jerry.

Censor – Censure

Censor means *to suppress, forbid or delete offensive material, especially officially*.

Example: All the vulgar movie scenes fell to censor cuts.

Censure denotes *the expression of severe disapproval of; to formally scold or reprove*.

Example: The actress' family members censured her for doing vulgar scenes in the movie.

Chary – Wary

Chary means to be *cautiously or suspiciously reluctant*.

Example: Most politicians are chary of poll reforms.

Wary denotes being *cautious about possible dangers or problems*.

Example: All politicians are wary of any suggestions for poll reforms.

In this instance, both words may still seem confusing (and interchangeable) after the meanings have been explained! Therefore, always remember that in *chary* the emphasis is on *carefulness, reserve and discretion*. In the case of wary, the stress is on *suspiciousness and keeping one's guard up against being cheated*.

Cite – Site

Cite means *quote (a book or author) to support an argument or as evidence; praise for a courageous act in an official communication.*

Example: Many instances of the jawan's bravery were *cited* when the award was presented to him.

Site denotes *an area of ground on which something is located, a place where a particular event or activity will occur or has occurred.*

Example: Shivaji Park is one of the best *sites* for large public meetings in the city of Mumbai.

Climactic – Climatic

Climactic denotes *forming an excellent climax.*

Example: The *climactic* scenes in the film were the best ever.

Climatic means *relating to the climate.*

Example: The *climatic* conditions in Delhi do not suit asthmatics.

Coarse – Course

Coarse denotes something that is *rough or harsh in texture; unrefined;* rude or vulgar (of a person or their behaviour).

Example: His behaviour in the presence of women is always *coarse*.

Course refers to *the route or direction followed by a vehicle, road or river, the way in which something progresses or develops.*

Example: Many rivers tend to follow a zigzag *course*.

Complacent – Complaisant

Complacent refers to a *feeling of smug and uncritically satisfaction with oneself or one's achievements.*

Example: The Australians were *complacent* when they played India in Australia and paid the price.

Complaisant denotes a *willingness to please others or accept their behaviour without protest.*

Example: The Pakistani team seemed *complaisant* when they faced India in the Friendship Series and were outplayed.

Complement – Compliment

Complement refers to a *thing that contributes extra features to something to improve or enhance it, the number or quantity that makes something complete.*

Example: Sonali Bendre's dresses *complement* her figure.

Compliment denotes *the polite expression of praise or admiration.*

Example: People always *compliment* Hema Malini for her sense of dignity.

Continual – Continuous

Continual denotes something that occurs *constantly* or *at frequent intervals.*

Example: There were *continual* infiltration attempts by the militants.

Continuous refers to something occurring *without interruption, non-stop.*

Example: For two hours, the Pakistanis indulged in *continuous* firing to aid the infiltration attempts of the militants.

Council – Counsel

Council refers to *a formally constituted body that is advisory, deliberative or administrative in nature, a body that is elected to run the affairs of a city or district.*

Example: The *council* looks after affairs of the city.

Counsel denotes *advice, particularly that given formally; a barrister or other legal adviser handling a case.*

Example: Do not offer your *counsel* unless you are asked specifically for it.

Crevasse – Crevice

Crevasse refers to *a deep open crack in a glacier or ice field.*

Example: While moving over a glacier, one must watch out for a *crevasse*.

Crevice denotes *a narrow opening or fissure, particularly in a rock or wall.*

Example: Every *crevice* in the mountains contains some minor forms of life.

****

Deduce – Deduct

Deduce denotes *to arrive at or to infer (a fact or conclusion) through reasoning or evidence.*

Example: The police were able to *deduce* that the foreign tourist had been killed for money.

Deduct means *to subtract or take away from a total.*

Example: A fine was *deducted* from Saurav Ganguly's match fees for India's slow over rate.

If you are still in doubt about differentiating between the two words, remember: *deduce* implies to put two and two together, while *deduct* would mean two minus two!

Definite – Definitive

Definite means *clearly stated or defined, not vague or doubtful.*

Example: There was a *definite* game plan to the prisoners' hostage-taking drama.

Definitive denotes *something (a conclusion or agreement etc.) that has been done or reached decisively and with full authority, something that is final and conclusive.*

Example: The prisoners came up with *definitive* demands for the release of the hostages.

Deprecate – Depreciate

In its strictest sense, to **deprecate** an action means *to express disapproval of; deplore.*

Example: All Patna citizens have *deprecated* the ransom kidnappings that are taking place regularly.

To **depreciate**, strictly speaking, means *to lessen the price or value of; to think and speak of as being of little value; to belittle.*

Example: Values of property in Patna have *depreciated* due to regular kidnappings for ransom.

However, thanks to the confusion between the two words, *deprecate* is now increasingly used in the sense of *to belittle* or *depreciate*.

Desert – Dessert

Desert means:

1. *To abandon callously or treacherously.*
2. *Leave a place, making it appear empty.*
3. *Illegally run away from military service.*
4. *A waterless, desolate area of land that is without usually without vegetation (or with very little) and is typically covered with sand.*

Example: Many youngsters now *desert* their parents when they group up, due to the negative influence of modern living.

Dessert refers to *the sweet dish eaten after a meal.*

Example: Custard-and-jelly is a popular after-dinner *dessert*.

Discomfit – Discomfort

Discomfit means *to make uneasy or embarrassed.*

Example: Some politicians were *discomfited* by the disclosures made by the CAG.

Discomfort denotes *slight pain, slight anxiety or embarrassment.*

Example: When politicians are jailed for their misdeeds, they are prone to *discomfort*.

Discreet – Discrete

Discreet means being *careful and prudent in one's speech or actions, particularly in order to avoid giving offence or attracting attention.*

Example: Unlike Shatrughan Sinha who shoots his mouth, Amitabh Bachchan uses his words in a *discreet* manner.

Discrete denotes being *individually separate and distinct.*

Example: The tasks given to both contestants were *discrete*.

Disinterested – Uninterested

Disinterested implies *not influenced by considerations of personal advantage, impartial.*

Example: GR Khairnar was always *disinterested* in the gains of office when he served the Brihanmumbai Municipal Corporation.

Uninterested means *not interested or concerned.* Many erroneously use *disinterested* when they mean *uninterested*.

Example: GR Khairnar was *uninterested* in personal safety when he took on land sharks in Mumbai.

Disburse – Disperse

Disburse denotes *pay out* (of money from a fund).

Example: The government must *disburse* village funds on time when there is a crisis.

Disperse means to *go or distribute in different directions or over a wide area, thin out and eventually disappear.*

Example: The officials *dispersed* in all directions to disburse the funds.

Dual – Duel

Dual refers to *something that consists of two parts, elements or aspects.*

Example: All people have a *dual* role to play in life – personal and professional.

Duel means *a contest between to parties to settle an issue* (modern usage); *a pre-arranged contest or fight between two people with deadly weapons to settle a dispute* (historical usage).

Example: In the old days, a person challenged his rival to a *duel* unto death to settle scores.

****

Emigrate – Immigrate

Emigrate denotes *the act of leaving one's country to settle down permanently in another country.*

Example: Many Indians have *emigrated* from India in search of a better future.

Immigrate means *come to live permanently in a foreign country.*

Example: Many Indians have *immigrated* to the US, Canada, Australia and New Zealand to seek their fortunes.

Enormity – Enormousness

Enormity refers to the *extreme seriousness of something, especially a crime.*

Example: Most serial killers like Charles Sobhraj fail to realise the *enormity* of their crimes.

Enormousness refers to *something that is very large*. However, *enormity* has now acquired the meaning of *enormousness* due to its regular incorrect usage.

Example: The *enormousness* of the tasks given to election officials is obvious.

Ensure – Insure

Ensure denotes *to make certain that something will be done or occur*.

Example: Every worker on the Delhi Metro has to *ensure* that his tasks are completed on time.

Insure means *to arrange for compensation if there is any damage to or loss of property, life or a person, in exchange for regular payments to a company*.

Example: It is always safe to *insure* one's car, house and other costly items.

Envelop – Envelope

Envelop means *to wrap up, cover or surround completely*.

Example: During winters, cities in north India are *enveloped* in mist.

Envelope denotes *a flat paper cover or container that is used to enclose a letter or document, which has a sealable flap*.

Example: It is better to use a dark-coloured *envelope* to despatch cheques or drafts.

Equable – Equitable

Equable means *calm or even-tempered, steady and uniform*.

Example: Very few countries have an *equable* climate.

Equitable denotes *fair, just and impartial*.

Example: If most states agreed to an *equitable* distribution of river waters, many inter-state problems would vanish.

Everyday – Every day

Everyday means *something that occurs daily or is routine and commonplace*.

Example: Fights between some couples are an *everyday* affair.

Every day denotes *something that happens every single day*.

Example: Not all couples fight *every day*.

****

Factious – Fractious
Factious means *relating or inclined to dissention, tending to promote internal strife through the formation of factions*.

Example: The formation of various groups within a political party has *factious* implications.

Fractious denotes (somebody or something) *easily irritated or difficult to control*.

Example: Some Bollywood superstars have *fractious* personalities.

Flaunt – Flout
Flaunt means to *display ostentatiously*.

Example: Teenage offspring of rich parents like to *flaunt* their wealth.

Flout denotes to *openly disregard a rule, law or convention*.

Example: Children of rich or powerful people like to *flout* the laws of the land.

Fortuitous – Fortunate
Fortuitous means *happening by chance rather than by design*.

Example: A few people make it big after securing a *fortuitous* break in life.

Fortunate means *favoured by or involving good luck*.

Example: Some people are very *fortunate* and repeatedly get good breaks in life.

****

Gamble – Gambol
Gamble means:
   1. *To play games of chance for money; bet.*
   2. *Take a risky action in the hope of a desired result.*

Example: Paradoxically, many unemployed persons love to *gamble*.

Gambol refers to the act of *running or jumping about playfully*.

Example: Mountain goats dare to *gambol* even on the edge of high mountain precipices.

Gild – Guild

Gild means:
1. *Cover thinly with gold.*
2. (**Adj. = gilded**) *wealthy and privileged.*

Example: As a child, he lead a *gilded* life.

Guild refers to *an association of people who come together for mutual aid or the pursuit of a common goal.*

Example: Most active journalists from the mainstream print and electronic media happen to be members of the Press *guild*.

****

Historic – Historical

Historic means *famous or important in history or potentially so* (a person, date or event).

Example: Chhatrapati Shivaji Maharaj's coronation is a *historic* day in Maratha and Indian history.

Historical denotes *of or concerning history.*

Example: The events of Shivaji Maharaj's life are truly of *historical* importance with reference to various freedom struggles in India.

****

Imply – Infer

Imply means *to indicate by suggestion rather than by direct reference, to hint or to insinuate.*

Example: The witness *implied* that there were more rioters involved in torching the bakery.

Infer means *to draw a conclusion or to deduce from evidence and reasoning rather than from explicit statements.*

Example: Despite the witness turning hostile, the judge *inferred* that the accused were present during the riots.

Inflammable – Inflammatory

Inflammable refers to *(something that is) easily set on fire.*

Example: All fuels, including CNG, are highly inflammable.

Inflammatory denotes (speech or action) *arousing or intended to arouse an angry or violent feeling or reaction.*

Example: Communal politicians are notorious for making *inflammatory* speeches.

Ingenious – Ingenuous

Ingenious means *clever, original, resourceful and inventive.*

Example: As a chess player, Mikhail Botvinnik was renowned for his *ingenious* moves under pressure.

Ingenuous denotes *innocent, artless, unsuspecting and naive.*

Example: Making *ingenuous* pawn moves will take a chess player nowhere.

Its – It's

Its means:
   1. *Belonging to or associated with a thing previously mentioned or easily identified.*
   2. *Belonging to or associated with a child or animal of unspecified sex.*

Example: The child ate *its* food with relish.

It's denotes:
   1. *It is.*
   2. *It has.*

Example: Honesty is the best policy and *it's* a sensible way to live life.

****

Judicial – Judicious

Judicial denotes *of, by or appropriate to a law court or judge.*

Example: The employees will decide their next course of action after the *judicial* review is out.

Judicious refers to *having or done with good or sound judgement.*

Example: When it comes to fine food, many French women are said to be extremely *judicious*.

****

Knead – Need
Knead denotes:
1. *Work (dough or clay) with the hands.*
2. *Massage as if kneading.*

Example: All employees at the bakery, whether male or female, have to be adept in the art of *kneading*.

Need means:
1. *Require something because it is essential or very important rather than simply desirable.*
2. *Expressing necessity or obligation* (usually with a negative or in question form).

Example: This is definitely not something that I want – it is rather something that I *need*.

****

Loose – Lose
Loose denotes *not fixed firmly or tightly in place; not fitting closely or tightly.*

Example: After I lost weight, all my clothes became *loose*.

Lose refers to something *characterised by luxury, indicating comfort and ease.*

Example: Many western countries have a *luxurious* standard of living.

Luxuriant – Luxurious
Luxuriant denotes *rich and profuse in growth (of vegetation) or thick and healthy (of hair).*

Example: Countries in the rain-shadow region are devoid of *luxuriant* crop cover.

Luxurious refers to something *characterised by luxury, indicating comfort and ease.*

Example: Many western countries have a *luxurious* standard of living.

****

Militate – Mitigate
Militate denotes to *work against, to hamper or hinder, fight against. Militate* is almost always followed by *against*.

Example: Terrorism always *militates against* every freedom struggle and is a counterproductive weapon.

Mitigate refers to *making (something) less severe, serious or painful, to make milder.*

Example: Proper development can *mitigate* many of the conditions and hardships that foster militancy.

****

Noisome – Noisy

Noisome means *having an extremely offensive smell; disagreeable or unpleasant.*

Example: Many persons, particularly small children, consider the radish a *noisome* vegetable.

Noisy denotes *something full of or making a lot of noise.*

Example: People from the 50-plus generation consider pop music to be an extremely *noisy* nuisance.

****

Official – Officious

Official denotes *having authoritative standing; of or relating to an authority or public body and its activities and responsibilities.*

Example: Only *official* holidays are allowed in some companies.

Officious means *to assert authority or interfere in an annoying manner and sometimes even going beyond official duties, domineering and bossy.*

Example: Some people like to throw their weight around and act so *officious*.

****

Peak – Peek

Peak denotes:
   1. *The pointed top of a mountain.*
   2. *The highest point of activity or achievement.*

Example: Has Sachin Tendulkar crossed the *peak* of his cricketing career?

Peek means:
1. *Look quickly or furtively.*
2. *To protrude or jut out slightly so as to be just visible.*

Example: Sachin Tendulkar's debut tour against Pakistan gave the world a *peek* of the batting genius that would soon blossom.

Perspicacity – Perspicuity
Perspicacity means *having a clear understanding about things.*

Example: *Perspicacity* helps a statesman solve most problems.

Perspicuity denotes *something that is clearly expressed and easily understood.*

Example: A solution that lacks *perspicuity* will be no solution.

Pore – Pour
Pore denotes:
1. *A minute opening in the skin or other surface.*
2. *To read closely or study carefully.*

Example: The detective *pored* over all the documents.

Pour means:
1. *Flow or cause to flow in a steady stream.*
2. *Come or go in a steady stream (of people or things).*

Example: The rain kept *pouring* heavily.

Principal – Principle
Principal denotes:
1. *Main or first in order of importance.*
2. *An original sum of money invested or lent.*
3. *The head of a school or college.*

Example: The *principal* aim in life is to do well.

Principle means:
1. *A fundamental truth or proposition that serves as the foundation for a belief or action; a rule or belief governing one's personal behaviour.*
2. *A fundamental source or the basis of something.*

Example: Honest people follow certain *principles* in life, irrespective of the consequences of their actions.

Prescribe – Proscribe

Prescribe means *recommend something as beneficial, advise and authorise the use of (a medicine or line of treatment), particularly in writing.*

Example: The best antidote one could *prescribe* to curb negativity and depression is meditation and relaxation.

Proscribe denotes *forbidding something, especially by law.*

Example: In dry states like Gujarat, liquor is proscribed.

****

Quiet – Quite

Quiet means:
1. *Making little or no noise, free from activity, disturbance or excitement.*
2. *Discreet, moderate or restrained.*

Example: *Quiet* waters are said to run deep.

Quite denotes:
1. *Completely, absolutely.*
2. *Fairly, moderately.*

Example: Are you *quite* certain that this river is not very deep?

****

Restive – Restless

Restive means:
1. *Unable to keep still or silent; restless.*
2. *(Of a horse or other animal) refusing to advance; stubbornly standing still or moving backwards or sideways.*

Example: When there were undeclared hostilities between India and Pakistan, troops on both sides of the border were in a *restive* mood.

Restless denotes *unable to relax or rest.*

Example: When the generals heard that war was likely to be declared any day between India and Pakistan, they were *restless* day and night.

****

Stationary – Stationery

Stationary means:
1. *Not moving.*
2. *Not changing in quantity or condition.*

Example: The train was *stationary* on the platform for over an hour.

Stationery denotes *paper and other materials required for writing*.

Example: This shop sells *stationery* items.

****

Than – Then

Than is used when:
1. *Introducing the second element in comparison.*
2. *Introducing an exception or contrast.*
3. *Expressions indicate one thing happening immediately after another.*

Example: Rather *than* cheat, it is better to study hard and pass.

Then denotes:
1. *At that time.*
2. *After that, next.*
3. *Therefore.*

Example: If the question paper is tough, *then* the best thing to do is answer only those questions you are sure about.

Their – They're

Their means:
1. *Belonging to or associated with the people or things previously mentioned or easily identified.*
2. *Belonging to or associated with a person of unspecified sex (used in place of 'his' or 'his or her'.*

Example: If you don't know who they are, how will you return *their* belongings?

They're denotes *they are*.

Example: If *they're* belongings have been found, you must return it to them.

Tortuous – Torturous

Tortuous means *full of twists and turns, winding and twisting*.

Example: The climb uphill to Vaishno Devi is steep and *tortuous*.

Torturous denotes *characterised by pain and suffering*.

Example: Despite the steep and tortuous climb to Vaisho Devi, thanks to sheer devotion, no devotee considers the trek *torturous*.

Troop – Troupe

Troop refers to:
   1. *Soldiers or members of the armed forces.*
   2. *A group of people or animals of a particular kind.*

Example: The *troops* maintained absolute silence in their forward march.

Troupe denotes *a group of actors, dancers or other entertainers who go touring to different venues*.

Example: Bollywood *troupes* make frequent trips to Dubai.

Turbid – Turgid

Turbid means *muddy, clouded and turbulent (of a liquid)*.

Example: It is difficult to swim in *turbid* waters.

Turgid denotes *swollen, inflated or pompous*.

Example: Some ancient languages today seem *turgid*.

****

Unexceptionable – Unexceptional

Unexceptionable refers to something that is *above objection, exception or reproach*.

Example: Some issues in Parliament are considered *unexceptionable*.

Unexceptional denotes something that is *ordinary, plain and not exceptional*.

Example: Most days in Parliament can be *unexceptional*.

****

Venal – Venial

Venal refers to *something that can be bought or bribed*.

Example: Most bureaucrats have *venal* tendencies.

Venial denotes *forgivable, excusable, pardonable or trivial* (a sin, fault or offence).

Example: Many people are prone to venial faults.

****

Who's – Whose

Who's refers to:
   1. *Who is*.
   2. *Who has*.

Example: *Who's* the best man to get this work done?

Whose denotes *belonging to or associated with which person, of whom or which*.

Example: *Whose* fault is it, if this work has not been done?

****

Your – You're

Your means:
   1. *Belonging to or associated with the person or people that the speaker is addressing.*
   2. *Belonging to or associated with any person in general.*
   3. *(With a capital 'Y') used when addressing the holder of certain titles.*

Example: *Your* vote is precious, so ensure you do not let it go waste.

You're denotes *you are*.

Example: *You're* the best person to ensure this job gets done.

○○

Revealing Prefixes

The heads or tails of anything do reveal a lot. Words are no exception. With some degree of certainty, the prefix of words can help us gauge what any word means, even if we are encountering it for the first time.

For instance, the prefix **Bi** denotes **two**. Therefore, all words beginning with **bi** would *likely* have a meaning connected to this sense. But do not forget that there are exceptions to every rule. Some rogue words with a particular prefix may buck this trend. Watch out for such words!

Ambi (Latin) = Both

Ambidextrous

Adj. *A person who is able to use the right and left hands with equal ease.*

Ambiguous

Adj. (Of language) *having more than one meaning or interpretation.*

Ambivalent

Adj. *Having mixed feelings or contradictory ideas about a thing or person.*

Ambivert

N. *A person who has a balance of extrovert and introvert features in his or her personality.*

Ante (Latin) = Before, preceding

Antecedent

N. 1. *A thing that existed before or logically precedes another.*
   2. (Antecedents) *a person's ancestors and social background.*

Adj. *Preceding in time or order.*

Antenatal
Adj. *Before birth; during or relating to pregnancy.*
N. *(Informal) a medical examination during pregnancy.*

Ante-room
N. *A small room leading to a main one, especially one serving as a waiting room; a large room in an officers' mess adjacent to the dining room.*

Arch(a)eo (Greek) = Old

Archaeology
N. *The study of human history and prehistory through the excavation of sites and the analysis of physical remains.*

Archaic
Ajd. *Very old or old-fashioned; belonging to an early period of art or culture.*

Auto (Greek) = Self

Autocracy
N. 1. *A system of government by one person with absolute power.*
   2. *A country, state or society governed in this way.*

Autocrat
N. 1. *A rule with absolute power.*
   2. *A domineering person.*

Auto-erotic
Adj. *Of or relating to sexual excitement generated by fantasising about or stimulating one's own body.*

Auto-suggestion
N. *Hypnotic or subconscious adoption of an idea which one has originated oneself.*

****

Bene (Latin) = Well

Benediction
N. *The utterance or bestowing of a blessing.*

Beneficent
Adj. *Doing good or resulting in good.*

Benevolent
Adj. 1. *Well meaning and kindly.*
    2. (Of an organisation) *serving a charitable cause.*

Benign
Adj. 1. *Friendly and kindly.*
    2. *Favourable, not harmful.*

****

Circum (Latin) = Around

Circumlocution
N. *The use of many words where fewer would do.*

Circumscribe
V. *Restrict, limit.*

Circumvent
V. *Find a way around* (an obstacle).

Contra, contro (Latin) = Against

Contrarian
N. *A person who opposes or rejects popular opinion, especially in stock exchange dealing.*

Contravene
V. *Offend against the prohibition or order of* (a law, treaty, etc), *conflict with.*

Controversy
N. *Disagreement, typically when prolonged or public.*

****

Dis (Latin) = Apart, away

Disconsolate
Adj. *Very unhappy, unable to be comforted.*

Discrepancy
N. *An illogical or surprising lack of compatibility or similarity between two or more facts.*

Disparate
Adj. *Essentially different in kind; not able to be compared.*

****

En (Greek) = In, into

Encaustic
Adj. *(In painting and ceramics) decorated by burning in colours as an inlay, especially by using coloured clays or pigments mixed with hot wax.*
N. *The art or process of encaustic painting.*

Encircle
V. *To form a circle around; surround.*

Enlist
V. *Enrol or be engaged in the armed forces.*

Epi (Greek) = Upon, near to, in addition

Epigram
N. *A concise and witty saying or remark; a short witty poem.*

Epigraph
N. 1. *An inscription on a building, statue or coin.*
   2. *A short quotation or saying at the beginning of a book or chapter, intended to suggest its theme.*

Epilogue
N. *A section or speech at the end of a book or play serving as a comment on or a conclusion to what has happened.*

Epitaph
N. *Words written in memory of a person who has died, especially as an inscription on a tombstone.*

Eu (Greek) = Well

Eugenics
Pl. N. *(treated as singular) The science of using controlled breeding to increase the occurrence of desirable inheritable characteristics in a population.*

Eulogy
N. *A speech or piece of writing that praises someone highly.*

Euphemism
N. *A mild or less direct or offensive word used in place of one that is harsh or blunt when referring to something unpleasant or embarrassing.*

Euphonious
Adj. *Sounding pleasant.*

End(o) (Greek) = Within

Endocrine
Adj. *(Physiology) of or denoting glands which secrete hormones or other products directly into the blood; pertaining to internal secretions.*

Ex (Latin) = Out, out of

Exorbitant
Adj. *(Of a price or amount) unreasonably; excessive.*

Exorcise
V. *To drive out (a supposed evil spirit) from a person or place.*

Extirpate
V. *To search out and destroy completely.*

Extrovert
N. 1. *An outgoing, socially confident person.*
   2. *(Psychology) a person primarily concerned with external things or objective considerations.*

Extra (Latin) = Beyond, outside of

Extrasensory
Adj. *By means other than through the known senses.*

Extravagant
Adj. 1. *Lacking restraint in spending money or utilising resources.*
   2. *Exceeding what is reasonable or appropriate.*

****

Hetero (Greek) = Unlike

Heterogeneous
Adj. 1. *Diverse in character or content.*
   2. *(Chemistry) denoting a process involving substances in different phases (solid, liquid or gaseous).*

Holo (Greek) = Wholly, entire, complete

Holocaust

N. *Destruction or slaughter on a mass scale.*

Holograph

N. *A manuscript that is handwritten by the author.*

Homo (Greek) = Like

Homologous

Adj. 1. Having the same relation, relative position or structure.

    2. (Biology) *Similar in position, structure and evolutionary origin (referring to organs).*

Hyper (Greek) = Above, beyond

Hyperbole

N. *Deliberate exaggeration not meant to be taken literally.*

****

Inter (Latin) = Between, among

Interpolate

V. 1. *Insert words in a book, especially to convey a false impression about its date.*

    2. *Interject (a remark) in a conversation.*

    3. (Mathematics) *insert (an intermediate term) into a series by estimating or calculating it from the surrounding known values.*

Intra (Latin) = Within

Intramural

Adj. *Occurring within the limits of a state, community, organisation or institution.*

Intro (Latin) = Within

Introspection

N. *The examination of one's own thoughts or feelings.*

Introvert

N. 1. *A shy, reticent person.*

    2. (Psychology) *a person predominantly concerned with his or her own thoughts and feelings.*

Adj. *Of, denoting or typical of an introvert.*

****

Macro (Greek) = Large

Macrocosm
N. 1. *The universe; the cosmos.*
   2. *The whole of a complex structure, especially that represented or epitomised in a small part of itself (a microcosm).*

Mega (Greek) = Great, large

Megalith
N. *(Archaeology) a large stone that forms a prehistoric monument or part of one.*

Megalomania
N. *Obsession with the exercise or control of power.*

Megaton
N. *A unit of explosive power equivalent to one million tons of TNT.*

Meta (Greek) = Across, beyond

Metamorphosis
N. 1. *A change in form or nature.*
   2. *(Zoology; in insects or amphibians) the process of transformation from an immature form to an adult form in two or more distinct stages.*

Metaphor
N. *A figure of speech wherein a word or phrase is used for something where it is not literally applicable; a thing meant to symbolise something else.*

Micro (Greek) = Small

Microcosm
N. 1. *Something that encapsulates in miniature form the characteristics of a thing much larger.*
   2. *Humankind regarded as the epitome of the universe.*

Multi (Latin) = Many

Multilingual
Adj. *In several languages or able to speak many languages.*

****

Neo (Greek) = New

Neologism
N. *A newly coined word or expression*

Neophyte
N. 1. *A person who is new to a subject, skill or belief.*
    2. *A novice in a religious order or a priest who is newly ordained.*

****

Omni (Latin) = All

Omnipotent
Adj. *Having unlimited or very great power (particularly in reference to a deity).*

Omnivorous
Adj. 1. *(Of an animal) feeding on a variety of food of both plant and animal origin.*
    2. *Indiscriminate in consuming or using whatever is available.*

****

Peri (Greek) = Around

Peripatetic
Adj. 1. *Travelling from place to place.*
    2. *Given to walking about while teaching* (also termed *Aristotelian*, derived from Aristotle's habit of walking to and fro while teaching).

Periphrastic
Adj. *In the habit of using indirect or circumlocutory speech or writing.*

Poly (Greek) = Many

Polyglot
Adj. 1. *Knowing or using several languages.*
    2. *(In reference to a book) having the text translated into several languages.*

Post (Latin) = After

Postscript

N. 1. An additional remark at the end of a letter, after the signature.

2. A sequel.

Pre (from Latin *prae*) = Before, in front of

Predilection

N. A preference, fondness or special liking for something.

N. 1. An action or event that serves as a prelude to something more important.

2. A piece of music that serves as an introduction.

3. The introductory part of a poem or other literary work.

Premeditate

V. Think out or plan an action beforehand (an action, especially a criminal one).

Pro (Greek) = Before, ahead

Prognosis

N. A forecast, especially one regarding the likely course of a disease or ailment.

Pseudo (Greek) = False

Pseudonym

N. A fictitious name, especially one that is used by an author.

****

Re, Retro (Latin) = Back, backward, again

Recapitulate

V. Summarise and state the main points again.

Recede

V. 1. Move back or further away.

2. Gradually diminish.

3. (Of a man's hair) cease to grow at the temples and above the forehead.

Retrogress
V. *Go back to an earlier and typically inferior state; engage in retrogression.*

****

Se (Latin) = Away, aside, apart

Secede
V. *Withdraw formally from membership of a federal union or a political or religious organisation.*

Seclude
V. *Keep someone away from other people.*

Sedulous
Adj. *Showing dedication and diligence.*

****

Trans (Latin) = Beyond

Transcend
V. 1. *Be or go beyond the range or limits of.*
   2. *To surpass.*

Trans (Latin) = Across

Transient
Adj. 1. *Lasting for a short time only.*
   2. *Staying or working in a place for a short time only.*

Transmigration
N. *The passing (of a soul) from one body to another after death.*

****

Ultra (Latin) = Beyond

Ultramundane
Adj. (Poetic or literary) *existing outside the known world or universe.*

Ultrasonic
Adj. *Of or involving sound waves with a frequency above the upper limits of human hearing.*

****

Vice (Latin) = In turn

Vicarious

Adj. 1. *Experienced only in imagination through the feelings or actions of another person.*

2. *Acting or done for another.*

Viceroy

N. *A ruler who exercises authority in a colony or protectorate on behalf of the sovereign.*

****

With (Anglo-Saxon) = Against

Withstand

V. 1. *Remain undamaged or unaffected.*

2. *Offer strong resistance or opposition to.*

****

Xeno (Greek) = Strange, foreign

Xenogamy

N. *(Botany) fertilisation of a flower by the pollen from a flower on a genetically different plant.*

Xenophobia

N. *Intense or irrational dislike or fear of people from other countries.*

Telltale Suffixes

Like prefixes, the suffix of words can help us gauge the meaning of many words, however esoteric it may sound.

For instance, the suffix **Cide** denotes **killing**. Therefore, all words ending with **cide** would have a meaning connected to this sense. Let us check out some popular suffixes, which will make our work all the more easier in understanding the roots, and thereby the meaning, of various words.

Archy (Greek *arkhein 'to rule'*) = Rule or government

Anarchy
N. A state of disorder due to lack of government or control.

Hierarchy
N. A system of ranking based on status or authority.

Matriarchy
N. 1. A system of society or government headed by women.
   2. A form of social organisation in which descent and relationship are decided through the female line.

Patriarchy
N. 1. A system of society or government headed by men.
   2. A form of social organisation in which descent and relationship are decided through the male line.

-Arium (Latin) = A place

Aquarium	= a tank for aquatic fauna and flora.
Columbarium	= a repository with niches for storing funeral urns.

Dolphinarium	=	an aquarium for dolphins.
Herbarium	=	a collection of dried plants.
Insectarium	=	a container for the study of insects.
Leprosarium	=	a leper hospital.
Oceanarium	=	a large seawater aquarium.
Planetarium	=	a domed building used to project images of the sky that displays the stars and planets.
Rosarium	=	a rose garden.
Sacrarium	=	the sanctuary of a church; a shrine.
Solarium	=	a room with sunbeds or sunlamps.
Termitarium	=	a termite colony.
Terrarium	=	a glass case for keeping small land animals, especially frogs and snakes.
Vivarium	=	an enclosure for keeping animals under observation.

****

Cide (Latin) = Kill, killer

A. Meaning *the killing of another.*

Aborticide	=	the killing of a foetus.
Amicide	=	the killing of a friend.
Brahminicide	=	the killing of a Brahmin.
Deicide	=	the killing of a god.
Episcopicide	=	the killing of a bishop.
Femicide	=	the killing of a woman.
Filicide	=	the killing of one's son or daughter.
Foeticide	=	the killing of a foetus.
Fratricide	=	the killing of one's brother or sister.
Genocide	=	the killing of a large number of people within a single population.
Gynaecide	=	the killing of a woman.
Hereticide	=	the killing of a heretic.
Hericide	=	the killing of a master.
Homicide	=	the killing of a person; murder.
Hospiticide	=	the killing of a guest or host.

Infanticide	=	the killing of a baby or infant.
Mariticide	=	the killing of a husband.
Matricide	=	the killing of a mother.
Nepoticide	=	the killing of a favourite.
Parenticide	=	the killing of a parent.
Parricide	=	the killing of a parent or other close relative.
Patricide	=	the killing of a father.
Prolicide	=	the killing of a one's own child.
Regicide	=	the killing of a king.
Senicide	=	the killing of an old person.
Siblicide	=	the killing of siblings in animal groups.
Sororicide	=	the killing of a sister.
Suicide	=	the intentional killing of oneself.
Tyrannicide	=	the killing of a tyrant.
Uxoricide	=	the killing of one's wife.
Vaticide	=	the killing of a foetus.

B. Meaning *a substance used to destroy plant or animal life*.

Acaricide	=	a substance used to kill mites or ticks.
Apicide	=	a substance used to kill bees.
Apricide	=	a substance used to kill boars.
Avicide	=	a substance used to kill birds.
Bacteride	=	a substance used to destroy bacteria.
Biocide	=	a substance used to kill living organisms.
Bovicide	=	a substance used to kill oxen.
Canicide	=	a substance used to kill dogs.
Cervicide	=	a substance used to kill deer.
Ceticide	=	a substance used to kill whales.
Cimicide	=	a substance used to kill bedbugs.
Culicicide/ imagicide	=	a substance used to kill mosquitoes.
Elephanticide	=	a substance used to kill elephants.
Felicide	=	a substance used to kill cats.
Floricide	=	a substance used to destroy flowers.
Formicicide	=	a substance used to kill ants.

Fungicide	= a substance used to destroy fungi.
Gallicide	= a substance used to kill fowl.
Gallinicide	= a substance used to kill chicken.
Germicide	= a substance used to kill germs.
Herbicide	= a substance used to destroy vegetation.
Herpicide	= a substance used to kill reptiles.
Hiricide	= a substance used to kill goats.
Hirudicide	= a substance used to kill leeches.
Insecticide	= a substance used to kill insects.
Larvicide	= a substance used to kill larva.
Lousicide/ pediculicide	= a substance used to kill louse.
Lupicide	= a substance used to kill wolves.
Macropocide	= a substance used to kill kangaroos.
Muricide	= a substance used to kill mice.
Muscacide	= a substance used to kill flies.
Ovicide	= a substance used to destroy eggs.
Pesticide	= a substance used to kill pests.
Piscicide	= a substance used to kill fish.
Pulicicide	= a substance used to kill fleas.
Raticide	= a substance used to kill rats.
Spermicide	= a contraceptive that kills spermatozoa.
Talpicide	= a substance used to kill moles.
Tauricide	= a substance used to kill bulls.
Ursicide	= a substance used to kill bears.
Vaccicide	= a substance used to kill cows.
Vermicide	= a substance used to kill worms.
Vespacide	= a substance used to kill wasps.
Vulpicide	= a substance used to kill foxes.

****

Fic (Latin) = From *facere*: make, do

Beatific

Adj. Feeling or expressing blissful happiness.

Soporific

Adj. Inducing drowsiness or sleep; sleepy.

****

Graphy (Greek *graphia*) = Writing

A. -Graphy words that are related to *writing*.

Calligraphy	= decorative handwriting.
Epigraphy	= the interpretation of ancient scriptures.
Hagiography	= a biography that idealises its subject.
Orthography	= spelling, especially incorrect spelling.
Palaeography	= the study of ancient handwriting.
Stenography	= writing and transcribing shorthand.
Typography	= the process of setting type; the style of printed matter.

B. -Graphy words related to *the production of images, graphs and diagrams*.

Macropocide	= a substance
Cartography	= the science of drawing maps.
Encephalography	= a technique for recording electrical activity in the brain.
Holography	= the production of three-dimensional images (holograms).
Lithography	= a printing process.
Mammography	= the use of X-rays to detect breast abnormalities.
Pornography	= writing and images that arouse sexual excitement and interest.
Radiography	= the production of images by X-rays, gamma rays etc.
Tomography	= a technique for producing an image showing a cross-section through the body.
Topography	= the arrangement of the physical features of an area.

C. -Graphy words meaning *a descriptive science or study*.

Cosmography	= the science of the universe.
Crystallography	= the science of crystals.
Ethnography	= the study of different peoples.

Geography	=	the study of the physical features of the earth and their relation to human populations.
Oceanography	=	the science of the sea.
Petrography	=	the study of rocks.

****

Gregis (Italian) = Herd

Aggregate
N. 1. A whole formed by combining several disparate elements.

2. The total score of a player or team in a fixture comprising more than one game or round.

Congregate
V. Gather into a crowd or mass.

Segregate
V. 1. To set apart from the rest or from one another.

2. Separate along racial, sexual or religious grounds.

****

-Ism (Greek via Latin) = Doctrine or system

Aphorism
N. *A concise statement containing wisdom or truth; a maxim; a saying.*

Altruism
N. Selfless concern for the well-being of others.

Jingoism
N. *Chiefly derogatory.* Extreme patriotism – particularly in the form of aggressive foreign policy.

****

-Ine (Latin) = Relating to

A. Mammals

Bovine	=	relating to cattle.
Canine	=	relating to dogs.
Caprine	=	relating to goats.
Equine	=	relating to horses.
Feline	=	relating to cats.
Leoine	=	relating to lions.

Leporine	= relating to hares.
Lupine	= relating to wolves.
Murine	= relating to mice or other rodents.
Ovine	= relating to sheep.
Phocine	= relating to the true seals.
Porcine	= relating to pigs.
Taurine	= relating to bulls.
Ursine	= relating to bears.
Vulpine	= relating to foxes.

B. Birds

Anserine	= relating to geese.
Aquiline	= relating to eagles.
Corvine	= relating to crows or ravens.
Hirundine	= relating to birds of the swallow family.
Passerine	= denoting perching birds.
Pavonine	= relating to peacocks.

****

Mania (Latin via Greek) = Madness

Anthomania	= a passion for flowers.
Bibliomania	= a passionate love for books.
Dipsomania	= a craving for alcohol; alcoholism.
Egomania	= obsessive egotism.
Erotomania	= obsessive sexual desire.
Kleptomania	= an irresistible urge to steal.
Megalomania	= an obsession with power.
Micromania	= a tendency to belittle oneself.
Monomania	= obsession with one thing.
Mythomania	= an abnormal tendency to tell lies.
Nymphomania	= uncontrollable sexual desire in a woman.
Pyromania	= obsessive desire to burn things.
Tulipomania	= obsession to possess tulips.

****

Ology (Greek *logos*) = Word, study, science

Entomology	= study of insect life.
Etymology	= science dealing with the origin and development of words and the study of their true meaning.
Indology	= the study of Indian history, literature, philosophy and culture.

****

-Onym (Greek) = Name

A. *Types of names.*

Anonym	= an anonymous person or thing.
Cryptonym	= a code name.
Eponym	= a name or word taken from a person's name.
Pseudonym	= a fictitious name, like that used by an author.
Toponym	= a place name.

B. *Words with a specific relationship to another word(s).*

Acronym	= a word formed from the initial letters of other words.
Antonym	= a word that has the opposite meaning to another.
Homonym	= each of two written words with the same written form but with different meanings and origins.
Meronym	= a term denoting part of something that is used to refer to the whole.
Metonym	= a word used to substitute for another.
Synonym	= a word or phrase with the same (or similar) meaning as another.

****

Osis (Greek) = A condition; a disease

Hypnosis

N. An artificially induced artificial state of consciousness, characterised by heightened suggestibility and receptivity to directions; a sleep-like condition.

Neurosis
N. A relatively mild mental illness not caused by organic disease, involving anxiety, depression, obsessive behaviour etc. but not a radical loss of touch with reality.

****

Phile (Greek *philos*) = Loving, lover of

Anglophile	= a person who is fond of or greatly admires England or Britain.
Audiophile	= a hi-fi enthusiast.
Bibliophile	= a lover of books.
Cinephile	= a person who loves cinema.
Extremophile	= an organism that lives in extreme environmental conditions.
Francophile	= a lover of France or French things.
Halophile	= an organism that thrives in salty conditions.
Logophile	= a person who loves words.
Necrophile	= a person who is sexually attracted to dead bodies.
Oenophile	= a wine connoisseur.
Paedophile	= a person who is sexually attracted to children.
Technophile	= a person who loves new technology.
Thermophile	= an organism that lives in hot temperatures.

****

Phobia (Greek) = Extreme or irrational fear or dislike

Acrophobia	= fear of heights or high places.
Agoraphobia	= fear of open or public places.
Ailurophobia	= fear of cats.
Arachnophobia	= fear of spiders.
Bibliophobia	= fear or dread of books.
Brontophobia	= fear of thunderstorms.
Claustrophobia	= fear of confined or closed places.
Cyberphobia	= fear of computer technology.
Deipnophobia	= fear of dinner parties.
Ergophobia	= fear of work.

Erythrophobia	=	intolerance of red colour.
Europhobia	=	hatred of Europe and the European Union.
Gynophobia	=	fear of women.
Homophobia	=	fear of homosexuality.
Hydrophobia	=	fear of water.
Islamophobia	=	irrational hatred or fear of Islam.
Logophobia	=	fear of words.
Mycophobia	=	fear of mushrooms.
Necrophobia	=	fear of death or dead bodies.
Neophobia	=	fear of the new or unfamiliar.
Nyctophobia	=	fear of night or darkness.
Panophobia	=	terror or excessive panic.
Photophobia	=	extreme sensitivity to light.
Psychrophobia	=	fear of cold things.
Technophobia	=	fear of new technology.
Thalassophobia	=	fear of the sea.
Triskaidekaphobia	=	fear or superstition regarding the number 13.
Tyrannophobia	=	fear of tyrants.
Xenophobia	=	fear or dislike of strangers or foreigners.

****

Wise (Anglo-Saxon) = Way or manner

Likewise

Adv. 1. Similarly.

    2. Also; moreover.

Otherwise

Adv. 1. In different circumstances; or else.

    2. In other respects.

    3. In a different way.

∞

Group Terms

The terms used for a group of people, animals or birds may not always be what you expect. Here are some group terms for various species that walk (or stalk) the earth. Some of the terms may have been used in medieval times. Others may have simply appeared in jocular usage, but never actually gained popular currency. However, all these words are being presented for the knowledge of readers who would care (or dare!) to use them.

Animal Terms

Name	Group Term
Antelopes	Herd
Apes	Shrewdness
Asses	Herd, pace
Badgers	Cete
Bears	Sloth, sleuth
Boars	Sounder
Bucks	Herd, leash
Buffaloes	Herd, gang
Camels	Flock
Cats	Clowder, glaring
Cattle	Herd, drove, drift, mob
Chamois	Herd
Colts	Rag, rake
Conies	Bury
Cubs	Litter
Curs	Cowardice

Deer	Herd, mob
Dogs	Pack, kennel
Dotterel	Trip
Elephants	Herd
Elks	Herd, gang
Ferrets	Business
Foxes	Earth, skulk
Giraffes	Herd
Goats	Herd, flock, trip
Hares	Drove, down, husk
Horses	Herd, harras, team
Hounds	Pack, leash, meet, mute, hunt
Kangaroos	Troop, mob
Kine	Drove
Kittens	Kindle
Leopards	Leap
Lions	Pride, troop
Mares	Stud
Martens	Richesse
Mice	Warren
Moles	Labour
Monkeys	Troop, tribe
Mules	Barren
Oxen	Herd, team, drove
Pigs	Litter, herd
Porpoises	School
Pups	Litter
Rabbits	Warren
Racehorses	Field, string
Rhinoceros	Crash
Roe deer	Bevy
Seals	Herd, rookery, pod
Sheep	Flock
Squirrels	Dray
Stoats	Pack

Swine	Sounder
Whelps	Litter
Wild cats	Dowt, destruction
Wolves	Pack, herd, route

****

Bird and Insect Terms

Name	**Group Term**
Ants	Swarm, nest
Bees	Hive, swarm, drift, bike
Birds	Flock, flight, congregation Volary (in an aviary)
Bitterns	Siege, sedge
Bustards	Flock
Chickens	Brood, clutch, peep
Choughs	Chattering
Coots	Covert
Cranes	Herd
Crows	Murder
Curlews	Herd
Doves	Flight, dole, piteousness
Ducks	Paddling (on the water) Team (in the air)
Dunlins	Flight
Eagles	Convocation
Finches	Charm
Flies	Cloud
Geese	Gaggle (on water), team, wedge Skein (in the air)
Goshawks	Flight
Grouse	Covey (single family) Pack (large group)
Gulls	Colony
Hawks	Cast
Hens	Brood

Herons	Siege, sedge
Hummingbirds	Charm
Insects	Flight, swarm
Jays	Band, party
Lapwings	Desert, deceit
Larks	Exaltation
Locusts	Cloud, flight, swarm
Magpies	Tidings
Mallards	Flush, sord
Nightingales	Watch
Parrots	Flock, company
Partridges	Covey
Peacocks	Brood (same family) Nye (large group)
Penguins	Colony, rookery
Pheasants	Head, nye
Pigeons	Flock, flight, kit
Plovers	Congregation, stand, wing
Pochards	Flight, rush
Poultry	Run
Ptarmigan	Covey
Quails	Bevy, drift
Ravens	Unkindness
Rooks	Building, clamour, parliament
Sheldrakes	Dopping
Snipe	Walk, wisp
Sparrows	Host
Starlings	Chattering, murmuration
Storks	Mustering
Swallows	Flight
Swans	Herd, game, or wedge (in the air)
Swifts	Flock
Teals	Knob, spring
Turkeys	Rafter

Widgeons	Flight (flying)
	Bunch, company, knob (on water)
Wildfowl	Plump, trip
Woodcock	Fall
Woodpeckers	Descent
Wrens	Herd

****

Fish and Amphibia Terms

Name	Group Term
Eels	Swarm
Dogfish	Troop
Fish	School, shoal
Frog	Army
Herring	Army, glean, shoal
Mackerel	Shoal
Minnows	Shoal
Perch	Shoal
Pilchards	Shoal
Porpoises	Herd, pod, school
Roach	Shoal
Sardines	Family
Sticklebacks	Shoal
Toads	Knot
Trout	Hover
Turtles	Bale
Whales	School, herd, pod, gam
Whiting	Pod

****

Human Terms

Name	Group Term
Aborigines	Tribe
Actors	Troupe, company

Admirals	Swell
Advisers	Council
Aldermen	Guzzle
Angels	Elongation
Announcers (radio)	Accent
Aunts	Anticipation
Autobiographers	Excess
Aviators	Celerity
Babies	Dampness
Bachelors	Debauchery
Bandsmen	Furore
Barbarians	Horde
Barbers	Botheration
Bathers (seaside)	Nudity
Beaters	Squad
Beauties	Galaxy
Beggars	Whine
Bishops	Bench, psalter, unction
Bookmakers	Surge
Boys	Blush, riot, rascal
Boy scouts	Troop, jamboree
Bursars	Cheat
Businessmen	Syndicate
Butchers	Bloodiness
Butlers	Draught
Canons	Dignity
Capitalists	Company, syndicate
Cavalry	Troop, squadron
Chauffeurs	Squirt
Children	Scamper
Clergymen	Assemblage, convocation
Clerks	Ledger
Clowns	Guffaw
Colonels	Blimp
Commissionaires	Chestiness

Communists	Envy
Constables	Posse
Convicts	Gang
Cooks	Burning, hastiness
Councillors	Syndicate
Cousins	Countryside
Cricketers	Grace
Curates	Charge, coyness
Damsels	Spray
Dancers	Troupe, clutter
Daughters	Dependence
Deans	Dread
Delegates	Congress
Dentists	Removal
Diplomats	Suavity
Directors	Board
Doctors	Emulsion
Dramatists	Dialogue
Editors (newspapers)	Erudition
Farmers	Grousing
Fathers	Fatuity, overdraft
Film stars	Screen
Financiers	Corner
Fishermen	Elongation
Followers	Train
Footballers (association)	Dribble
Footballers (rugby)	Tackle
Foresters	Stalk
Gardeners	Growth
Generals	Importance
Girls	Bevy
Golfers	Foozle, bogey
Gossips	Gaggle
Grocers	Imposition
Harpers	Melody

Hermits	Observance
Highbrows	Altitude
Hikers	Hustle
Hooligans	Gang
Housewives	Duster
Hunters	Blast, hunt, meet
Husbands	Duty
Inspectors	Panel
Journalists	Column
Judges	Bench, panel
Kings	Dynasty
Knaves	Rayful
Labourers	Gang
Ladies	Bevy
Lawyers	Surplus
Learned men	School
Loafers	Saunter
Lovers (female)	Delight
Lovers (male)	Flattery, cornucopia
Lowbrows	Earthiness
Magistrates	Bench
Majors	Morbidity
Members of Parliament	Chatter, promise
Merchants	Caravan, company, syndicate
Milkmaids	Galaxy
Milkmen	Clatter
Millionaires	Mammon
Miners	Muttering
Minstrels	Troupe
Misers	Proximity
Mothers	Patience
Motorists	Licence, mania
Musicians	Band
Navvies	Neckerchief
Nurses	Cuddle

Oarsmen	Crew
Officials	Staff
Optimists	Micawber
Pacifists	Propaganda
Pedestrians	Morgue
Peeping Toms	Godiva
People	Crowd, throng, multitude, group
Persons	Class
Philosophers	Frowst
Pilgrims	Caravan
Players	Team
Playwrights	Cast
Plumbers	Procrastination
Poets	Gush, afflatus
Policemen	Draft, posse
Politicians	Caucus
Postmen	Delivery
Princes	State
Principals	Lac
Prisoners	Gang, pity
Proctors	Prowl
Publishers	Optimism
Rascals	Parcel
Relatives	Invasion
Religious people	Sect
Representatives	Congress
Robbers	Band, gang
Rulers	Dynasty
Sailors	Crew, watch
Saints	Community
Savages	Horde
Schemers	Clique
Scholars	Collation
Scientists	Quantum

Senators	House
Sergeants	Subtlety
Servants	Staff
Shopkeepers	Nation
Shoppers	Press
Singers	Choir
Slaves	Gang
Socialists	Heckle
Soldiers	Boast, draft
Sons	Independence
Spinsters	Flutter
Statesmen	Pact
Students	Class
Subalterns	Simplicity
Surgeons	Seesaw
Tailors	Long credit
Taxi drivers	Expectation
Telephone operators	Apology
Thieves	Gang, skulk
Thinkers	School
Tourists	Drove
Travellers	Caravan
Typists	Tattoo
Tyrants	Egotism
Uncles	Disappointment
Urchins	Mischief
Vicars	Vicariousness
Virgins	Trace
Volunteers	Corps
Waiters	Dawdling
Wives	Questionnaire
Women	Bevy, gaggle (derogatory)
Workmen	Gang
Worshippers	Congregation
Writers	Sufficiency

Young people	Superiority
Zealots	Preachment

****

Sundry Terms

Name	Group Term
Aeroplanes	Flight
Arms	Pile
Arrows	Quiver
Beer	Brew
Bells	Carillon, peal
Bicycles	Wobble
Boats	Flotilla
Books	Library
Bread	Batch, caste
Bricks	Pile
Bullets	Shower
Cars	Fleet
Cards	Pack
Carriages	Train
Chairs	Row
China	Service
Cigars	Box
Cigarettes	Packet
Clothes	Outfit, suit, bundle
Cocktails	Shake, scatter
Coins	Collection
Cotton	Bale
Crockery	Service
Curiosities	Collection
Eggs	Clutch, laughter
Firewood	Bundle
Flowers	Bunch, posy, nosegay
Fruit trees	Orchard
Furniture	Suite

Gold	Hoard
Goods	Stock, consignment
Grapes	Bunch, cluster
Grass	Tuft
Hair	Lock, fell
Hay	Bundle
Hills	Range
Islands	Group, cluster
Keys	Bunch
Laws	Code
Leaves	Fall
Letters	Budget
Lies	Tissue
Machineguns	Nest
Money	Hoard
Mountains	Range
News	Budget
Nuts	Cluster
Onions	Rope
Papers	Sheaf
Pearls	Rope, string
Peas	Pod
Photos	Album
Pictures	Gallery
Plantains	Bunch
Poems	Anthology
Rain	Fall, shower
Rays	beam
Relics	Collection
Rooms	Suite
Roses	Bevy
Ruins	Heap, mass
Sails	Outfit
Sand	Heap
Sausages	Sizzle

Ships	Fleet
Silk	Skein
Snow	Fall
Stairs	Flight
Stamps	Collection, album
Stars	Constellation, galaxy, cluster
Sticks	Bundle, faggot
Stones	Heap, pile
Strawberries	Punnet
Tools	Set
Trees	Clump, thicket
Twigs	Faggot
Wagons	Train
Whisky	Case, want
Wine	Case
Wood	Pile
Wool	Bale, skein

∞

Some Commonly Misspelled Words

Spelling some words can be a major problem for most people not well versed with the English language. Such words can be really tricky (or is that *trickey*?). Here is a list of words commonly misspelled with their **correct spellings**.

Abattoir
Abbot
Aberration
Abeyance
Abdicate
Abhorrence
Ablution
Abolition
Abscess
Absence
Absorption
Abysmal
Abyss
Abundance
Academically
Accede
Accelerator
Accessible
Accessory
Accidentally

Acclaim
Acclimatise
Accommodate
Accompanist
Accomplish
Accordion
Accumulate
Achievement
Acknowledge
Acolyte
Acoustics
Acquaintance
Acquiesce
Acquittal
Across
Acute
Address
Adherent
Adjacent
Adjective

Administrable
Admiralty
Adolescent
Adrenalin
Adultery
Advantageous
Advertisement
Aegis
Aeon
Aerial
Aerobic
Aerodrome
Aesthetic
Affidavit
Aggravate
Aide-de-camp
Algebraic
Alignment
Alleged
Allegiance
Alliance
Alliteration
Allotting
Almanac
Already
Altogether
Amateur
Ambassador
Ambidextrous
Ancillary
Aneurysm
Angle

Annihilate
Annual
Annul
Anomalous
Antagonist
Antechamber
Antediluvian
Antithesis
Apartheid
Apparatus
Apparent
Appearance
Appositive
Archaeology
Archetype
Argument
Arraign
Asafoetida
Ascend
Asinine
Asphalt
Assassin
Assessment
Assonance
Asterisk
Atheist
Athletics
Attendance
Auxiliary
Awesome
Awfully

****

B

- Bachelor
- Ballet
- Balloon
- Bandoleer
- Bankruptcy
- Barbarian
- Barbaric
- Barbecue
- Barbiturate
- Bargain
- Baritone
- Basically
- Battalion
- Bazaar
- Beautiful
- Beggar
- Belligerence
- Beginning
- Behaviour
- Believe
- Beneficent
- Beneficial
- Benevolent
- Besiege
- Biased
- Bilingual
- Biscuit
- Bisect
- Bizarre
- Blasphemy
- Blitzkrieg
- Bluish
- Bologna
- Bookkeeper
- Bouillon
- Boulevard
- Boundary
- Bourgeois
- Boycott
- Bracelet
- Brethren
- Brier
- Britain
- Buddha
- Buffet
- Buoyant
- Bureaucrat
- Burial
- Business

****

C

- Cafeteria
- Cagey
- Calcium
- Calculation
- Calendar
- Calligraphy
- Calorie
- Camaraderie
- Camouflage
- Canalise
- Cancellation
- Candidate

Cannabis
Cantaloupe
Caramel
Caravan
Caravanserai
Carburettor
Carcass
Cardamom
Caribbean
Caricature
Carpentry
Cartographer
Casualty
Cataclysm
Catalyst
Catapult
Catarrh
Catastrophe
Category
Caucus
Cauldron
Cellar
Cemetery
Centenarian
Centred, centring
Centimetre
Chagrined
Challenge
Chameleon
Changing
Chaperon
Characteristic
Charge d'affaires
Chassis
Chastise

Chauffeur, chauffeuse (feminine)
Chequered
Chief
Chilli
Chlorophyll
Chocolate
Chockfull
Chord
Chrome
Chromosome
Chunky
Cigarette
Cinnamon
Cinderella
Cipher
Circuitous
Circumference
Circumstantial
Cirrhosis
Citizen
Clamour, clamorous
Clarinettist
Cliché
Climbed
Cliques
Coefficient
Coherence
Coincide
Collectible
Collision
Colonel
Colony
Colossal
Columbia

Column
Coming
Commemorate
Commission
Committal
Committee
Commitment
Commutative
Comparative
Compatible
Compelled
Competent
Competition
Complementary
Completely
Complexion
Composite
Comptroller
Concede
Conceive
Condemn
Condescend
Conferred
Congratulations
Congruent
Conjunction
Conjuror
Connoisseur
Conscientious
Consciousness
Consensus
Consequences

Consistent
Consolidator
Consonance
Consumer
Consummate
Continuous
Contraction
Controlled
Convalescent
Convener
Coolly
Corollary
Controversial
Convenient
Correlate
Correspondence
Counsellor
Courteous
Courtesy
Cricketer
Criticism
Criticise
Crucifixion
Cruelty
Curriculum
Curtail
Curtsy
Cyclical
Cylinder
Cymbal
Cyst

****

D

Dachshund
Dais
Daughter
Debacle
Debonair
Decadent
Decagon
Deceive
Decibel
Decimate
Deducible
Defendant
Deferential
Deferred
Definite
Deleterious
Demeanour
Denouement
Dependant (noun)
Dependent (adjective)
Depose
Depreciate
Deprecate
Dereliction
Descend
Descendant
Description
Desirable
Despair
Desperate
Desiccate
Detenu, detenue (feminine)
Detente

Detrimental
Devastation
Develop
Development
Dextrous/dexterous
Diagonal
Diameter
Diarrhoea
Dictionary
Dietician
Diesel
Difference
Dignitary
Dilemma
Dilettante
Diligence
Dimension
Diminution
Dining
Diphtheria
Disassemble
Disappearance
Disappoint
Disastrous
Discipline
Discreet
Discretion
Discrimination
Disease
Disdainfully
Disfranchise
Disguise
Dispel

Dispensable
Dissatisfied
Dissemination
Dissension
Disservice
Dissociate
Distinguish
Diversified
Doctrinaire
Dominant

Dormitory
Dormouse
Dovecot
Dullness
Duress
Drugged
Drunkenness
Dyeing
Dysentery
Dyspepsia

****

E

Earthen
Easily
Eccentric
Economy
Ecosystem
Ecstasy
Eczema
Edgeways
Educationist
Effervesce
Efficiency
Eighth
Either
Eligible
Electrolyte
Elegy
Elevation
Eligible
Eliminate
Ellipsis
Embalmment
Embarkation

Embarrass
Embezzlement
Emigrate
Eminent
Emperor
Emphasise
Empire
Employee
Empty
Enamel
Encouragement
Encrust
Encyclopaedia
Endeavour
Endemic
Enemy
Ennui
Enormous
Enrol
Enthral
Enthusiastically
Entrepreneur

Entirely
Entrance
Epaulette
Epidemiologist
Equality
Equator
Equestrian, equestrienne (feminine)
Equilibrium
Equipped
Equivalent
Erector
Escutcheon
Eulogise
Euthanasia
Especially
Espionage
Espresso
Essential
Exaggerate
Exceed
Excellence
Excellent
Excess

Excerpt
Excommunicate
Exercise
Exhaustion
Exhibition
Exhilarate
Exhort
Exhume
Exorbitant
Expansion
Existence
Expense
Experience
Experiment
Explanation
Exponent
Expression
Extempore
Extinct
Extort
Extraneous
Extremely
Extrovert
Exuberance

****

F

Facsimile
Factor
Facial
Faecal, faeces
Fahrenheit
Fallacious
Fallacy
Familiar

Fantasy
Fascinate
Fascism
Favourite
Feasible
Federation
Feisty
Felicity

Femininity
Fiancé, fiancée (feminine)
Fictitious
Filibuster
Fillip
Finally
Financially
Financier
Fiscal
Fission
Fisticuffs
Flautist (**not** flutist)
Fledgling
Floatation, flotation
Fluent
Fluorescent
Flyer
Foetus, foetal
Forbid
Forebode
Forcibly

Forecast
Foresee
Foretell
Forestall
Foreword
Forgather
Foreign
Forfeit
Formerly
Foresee
Formula
Forty
Fourth
Frantically
Frequently
Frieze
Fudge
Fulfil
Fundamentally
Fusillade

****

G

Gaiety
Gaily
Galaxy
Gamma
Garlic
Gaseous
Gauge
Gazetteer
Genealogy
Generalissimo
Generally

Genius
Geography
Glamour, glamorous
Gluing
Glycerine
Government
Governor
Grammatically
Gramophone
Granddaughter
Grandeur

Grandiloquent
Graphic
Gratuitous
Grey
Grievous
Grizzly
Grocery

Guarantee
Guerrilla
Guidance
Guillotine
Gypsy
Gyration

****

Haemorrhage
Haemorrhoids
Handicapped
Handkerchief
Happily
Harangue
Harass
Hare-brain
Harelip
Hartebeest
Height
Heinous
Heist
Hereabouts
Heredity, hereditary
Heterogeneous
Heritage
Heroes
Hesitancy
Hexagon
Hiccup
Hieroglyphics
Hindrance
Hippie
Hippopotamus

Hirsute
Hoarse
Holocaust
Homily
Homeopathy, homoeopathy
Homogenous
Honorific
Hoping
Horizontal
Horsy
Hospital
Hubbub
Hullabaloo
Humour, humorist, humorous
Hurrah (**not** hooray)
Hygiene
Hyperbole
Hypochondria
Hypocrisy
Hypocrite
Hypotenuse
Hypothesis

****

I

Ideally
Identikit
Ideological
Idiom
Idiomatic
Idiosyncrasy
Ignorance
Illogical
Imaginary
Imitate
Immediately
Immigration
Immolate
Immortal
Impeccable
Implement
Impostor
Impresario
Impugn
Inadvertent
Inaudible
Incidentally
Incredible
Independence
Independent
Indicted
Indigenous
Indispensable
Individually
Inequality
Inequitable
Inevitable
Inflammatory, inflammation
Inflexion
Influential
Information
Ingenious
Initially
Initiative
Innocent
Innocuous
Inoculate
Insistent
Insouciant
Install, instalment
Instantaneous
Instil
Institution
Insurance
Insurgency
Intellectual
Intelligence
Intelligentsia
Intercede
Interfered
Interference
Interjection
Interminable
Intermittent
Interregnum
Interrogate
Interrupt
Intricate
Introduce
Introvert
Invertebrate

Intuition	Irresistible
Intransigent	Irony
Inure	Irrelevant
Inveigh	Irresistible
Inveigle	Irritable
Investor	Island
Invigorate	Isosceles
Irascible	Itinerary
Iridescent	Isthmus

****

J

Jealousy	Judicial
Jewellery	Judicious
Journalism	Jugular
Judgment, judgement	

****

K

Kaleidoscope	Kinetic
Kerosene	Knead
Kiddie	Knowledge, knowledgeable
Kilometre	Kosher
Kindergarten	Kowtow

****

L

Laboratory	Lapse
Laborious	Largesse
Labyrinth	Larynx
Lachrymose	Latish
Lackadaisical	Latitude
Lackey	Latrine
Lambaste	Legerdemain
Lapis lazuli	Legionnaire

Legitimate
Leisure
Length
Lenient
Liaison
Library
Licence
Linchpin
Lieutenant
Lightning
Likelihood
Likely
Limerick
Lineage
Liquefy

Liquorice
Literati
Literature
Litterateur
Llama
Lodestar, lodestone
Longitude
Loneliness
Loquacious
Lose
Losing
Lounge
Lovely
Luxury
Lyric

****

M

Mackintosh
Maelstrom
Magazine
Magistrate
Magnificence
Mainland
Maintain
Maintenance
Malicious
Manageable
Manoeuvre
Manufacture
Marijuana
Mariner
Marquis
Marriage
Martyrdom
Mass

Mathematics
Mauve
Meadow
Meagre
Mean
Meanness
Median
Medicine
Medieval
Mediocre
Mediterranean
Melancholy
Melodious
Metallic
Memento
Metaphor
Meteorology

Mezzanine
Mien
Migratory
Mileage
Millennium
Milligram
Mimicry
Millipede
Millionaire
Miniature
Minuscule
Minutes
Mischievous
Misdemeanour
Missile
Misspelled
Mofussil

Monastery
Monarchy
Monetary
Moneyed
Montessori
Mortgage
Mosaic
Mosquito
Mosquitoes
Mundane
Munificent
Murmur
Muscle
Myriad
Mysterious
Myth
Mythology

****

Nadir
Naïve
Naphtha
Narcissism
Narrative
Nationalism
Naturally
Necessary
Necessity
Negligee
Neighbour
Nephew
Neurone
Neurotic
Neutral

Neutron
Niece
Nineteen
Ninety
Ninth
Nosey
Noticeable
Novelist
Nowadays
Nuclear
Nucleus
Nugatory
Nuisance
Nutrition
Nutritious

****

O

Oasis	Ophthalmology
Obedience	Opinion
Obelisk	Opossum
Oblivious	Opponent
Obsequies	Opportunity
Obsolete	Oppose
Obstacle	Opposition
Obtuse	Oppression
Occasion	Opprobrium
Occasionally	Optimism
Occurred	Orang-utan
Occurrence	Organdie
Octagon	Orchid
Oculist	Ordinarily
Official	Origin
Omelette	Originate
Omission	Oscillate
Omit	Outrageous
Omitted	Overrun
Onomatopoeia	Oxymoron
Opaque	

****

P

Paediatric	Paraffin
Pageant	Parakeet
Pamphlet	Parallel
Panegyric	Paralysis
Panicky	Paralyse
Panorama	Paranoia
Pantograph	Parcelled
Paradox	Parenting

Parliament
Parolee
Particularly
Partisan
Pastime
Patronage
Pavilion
Peaceable
Peasant
Peccadillo
Peculiar
Pedestal
Peddler
Peers
Penetrate
Pencilled
Penicillin
Peninsula
Pentagon
Perceive
Performance
Perimeter
Permanent
Permissible
Permitted
Perpendicular
Perseverance
Persistence
Personal
Personnel
Perspiration
Persuasion
Pessimistic
Pharaoh
Pharmaceutical

Phenomenon
Philanthropy
Philippines
Philosophy
Phoney
Phosphorus
Physical
Physician
Picnicking
Piece
Piggyback
Pilgrimage
Pitiful
Pixie
Pizzazz
Placebo
Plagiarism
Plagiarise
Plague
Planning
Plausible
Playwright
Pleasant
Plebiscite
Pneumonia
Pneumatic
Poliomyelitis
Politburo
Politician
Polygon
Polyhedron
Pomegranate
Portentous
Portray
Portuguese

Possess
Possessive
Possibility
Postscript
Potassium
Potato
Potatoes
Practically
Practice (noun),
practise (verb)
Practitioner
Prairie
Precede
Precedence
Precipitation
Precision
Precocious
Predicate
Preference
Preferred
Prefix
Prehistoric
Prejudice
Premier
Premiere
Preparation
Preposition
Prescription
Presence
Prestige
Presumption
Pretension
Pretentious
Prevalent

Primeval
Primitive
Prism
Privilege
Probability
Probably
Probation
Procedure
Proceed
Processor
Professor
Proffer
Prognosis
Proletariat
Prominent
Pronounce
Pronunciation
Propaganda
Propagate
Proprietary
Proprietor
Protagonist
Protein
Proximity
Psalm
Pseudonym
Psychoanalysis
Psychology
Psychiatrist
Publicly
Pummelled
Pursue
Putrefy
Puzzling

Pygmy
Pyjamas
Pyramid

Pyorrhoea
Pyrrhic
Pyrotechnics

****

Q

Quadrant
Quadrilateral
Quadruple
Qualify
Qualms
Quandary
Quantity
Quarantine
Quarrelled
Quell
Quench
Querulous
Query

Quest
Questionnaire
Queue
Quibble
Quiescent
Quinine
Quintessentially
Quipster
Quirk
Quizzes
Quorum
Quotation
Quotient

****

R

Radioactive
Rampage
Rampant
Rampart
Rapprochement
Rarefaction
Rarefy
Ratio
Reforestation
Realistically
Realise
Realtor
Rebellion

Rebut, rebuttal
Recede
Receipt
Receive
Recession
Recipient
Reciprocal
Recognise
Recommend
Recompense
Reconnaissance
Reconnoitre
Redress

Reference
Referred
Reflections
Refraction
Regiment
Rehearsal
Reign
Reimburse
Reincarnation
Relevant
Relieving
Religious
Remembrance
Reminiscence
Renaissance
Rendezvous
Renounce, renunciation
Repellent
Repetition
Repercussion
Representative
Resemblance
Reservoir

Resistance
Restaurant
Restaurateur
Resume
Resuscitate
Resurrection
Retaliate
Retrospect
Reveal
Revocation
Rhapsody
Rheumatism
Rhombus
Rhyme
Rhythm
Rhythmical
Rickety
Ridiculous
Rigour
Roommate
Rotary
Rotations

****

S

Sacrifice
Sacrilegious
Safari
Safety
Salami
Salary
Salutary
Sanatorium
Sandwich

Sanitise
Sarcasm
Satellite
Satire
Saturate
Savannah
Scallop
Scallywag
Scary

Scenery
Sceptical
Schedule
Scholastic
Scrimmage
Sebaceous
Secede
Secession
Secretary
Sediment
Segregate
Seismic
Seismograph
Seize
Sensitive
Sensory
Sentence
Sentry
Separate
Septuagenarian
Sequence
Sergeant
Serpent
Several
Severe
Shady
Shaky
Shameful
Shanghai
Shepherd
Sherbet
Sheriff
Shining
Shish kebab
Shrapnel

Shrewd
Siege
Significance
Simian
Similar
Simile
Simply
Sincerely
Singe
Siphon
Situation
Skiing
Skilful
Skimp
Skulduggery
Sleight
Smoky
Sober
Soliloquy
Solvent
Sombre
Somersault
Sophomore
Souvenir
Sovereign, sovereignty
Snorkel
Spasmodic
Specifically
Specimen
Spectre
Sphere
Sphinx
Sponsor
Spontaneous, spontaneity
Spoonful
Staccato

Stalemate	Supersede
Stamen	Supervisor
Statistics	Supplementary
Statue	Supposed
Statutory	Supposition
Stereophonic	Suppress
Stimulus	Surprise
Stopped	Surround
Straitjacket	Susceptible
Strait-laced	Suspicious
Strategy	Sustenance
Strength	Suzerain, suzerainty
Strenuous	Swedish
Stubbornness	Sweetmeat
Studying	Swelter
Stupefy	Sycamore
Stupor	Sycophant
Stymie	Syllable
Subcontinent	Sylvan
Submersible	Symbolic
Subordinate	Symmetrical
Subtle	Sympathy
Succeed	Symphonic
Success	Synchronise
Succession	Syncopation
Sufficient	Syndrome
Summary	Synonymous
Superannuate	Synopsis
Supercilious	Synthesise
Superintendent	Syringe

****

T

Tachometer
Taciturn
Talkative
Tangent
Tangible
Tapestry
Tariff
Tarpaulin
Taxiing
Technical
Technique
Technology
Temperamental
Temperature
Tenant
Tendency
Terminator
Terrain
Tertiary
Themselves
Theology
Theoretical
Theories
Therefore
Thermal
Thermodynamic
Threshold
Thesaurus
Thorough
Though
Thought
Through
Till
Tolerance
Tomorrow
Tortoise
Tournament
Tourniquet
Traffic, trafficking
Tragedy
Tranquil, tranquillity
Transatlantic
Transcend
Transferred
Transitory
Transparent
Trapezoid
Tremor
Trespass
Trough
Trousers
Truly
Tuition
Tumour
Tumultuous
Twelfth
Tyranny
Tyro

****

Ukulele
Unanimous
Undoubtedly
Universal
Unmistakable
Unnatural
Unnecessary
Unscrupulous

Unskilful
Until
Unwieldy
Usage
Usually
Utterance
Utopian

****

Vaccination
Vaccine
Vacillate
Vacuum
Vagabond
Valorous
Valedictory
Valuable
Variation
Vaudeville
Vehicle
Vendor
Veneer
Vengeance
Ventilate
Ventriloquist
Venue
Veracity

Veranda
Vermillion
Versatile
Vestige
Veterinary
Vicious
Vigilant
Vilify
Village
Villain
Vinegar
Violence
Visage
Visible
Visor
Voluminous
Voyeur

****

W

Wholesome	Warrant
Wholly	Warring
Wildebeest	Warrior
Wilful	Watt
Withhold	Weather
Woollen	Wednesday
Wolves	Weird
Woman	Welcome
Wreak	Wherever
Writing	Whether
Written	Whisper
Wrongful	Whistle
Wrung	Whittling
Wry	

****

X

Xanadu	Xenophobic
Xylophone	

****

Y

Yacht	Yeah
Yawn	Yield
Yea	Yuppie

****

Z

Zenith Zephyr	Zoology
Zinnia	Zucchini
Zigzag	
Zodiac	

Reticent Abbreviations

Many words are very popular in their abbreviated forms, so much so that before long people tend to forget the full form of the word. However, in order to have a good command over the English language, it is essential that you know the full form of all abbreviated words. This chapter gives abbreviations that are either commonly used or are common in a particular field of activity.

Another dilemma that readers may face is whether to write abbreviations with or without full stops. Nowadays, abbreviations are increasingly being spelt without full stops when the words in question are spelt with all capital letters (AGM, TTE, VIP) or a mix of capital and small letters (BSc, Ms). But full stops are almost always used when the word is made up entirely of small letters (p.a., a.m., p.m.), since they are less easily recognisable as abbreviations rather than words in this form. Shortened words or abbreviations consisting of the first few letters of words are generally spelt with a final full stop (co., Sept.). But those words where the abbreviation ends with the last letter of the word do not require a full stop (Dr, Dept, Mr, Mrs).

Finally, if an abbreviation with a full stop occurs at the end of a sentence, another full stop is never added if the full stop of the abbreviation is the last character.

A

AA	Alcoholics Anonymous
ABC	Audit Bureau of Circulation
ABM	Anti-ballistic missile
a.c.	Alternating current (electricity)

a/c	Account (banking)
AD	Anno Domini (in the year of our Lord; dating from the birth of Jesus Christ)
ADC	Aide-de-camp (helper or assistant)
Ad/advt	Advertisement
AG	Attorney-General
AGM	Annual General Meeting
AH	Anno Hegirae (Prophet Mohammed's flight from Mecca to Medina, AD 622; used before dates in Muslim history)
AIDS	Acquired Immuno-Deficiency Syndrome
AM	Ante Meridiem (before noon); Amplitude Modulation (radio)
Anon	Anonymous
A-1	First class
AP	Associated Press
Apr.	April
ASAP	As soon as possible
ATC	Air Traffic Control
ATM	Automatic Teller Machine
AV	Audio-visual
AWACS	Airborne Early Warning and Control System
AWOL	Absent without leave

****

B

b.	Born; bowled (cricket)
BA	Bachelor of Arts; British Airways
B&B	Bed and breakfast
BBS	Bulletin Board Service
BBC	British Broadcasting Corporation
BC	Before Christ
BCG	Bacillus Calmette Guerin (anti-TB vaccine)
B.Com.	Bachelor of Commerce
BDS	Bachelor of Dental Surgery

B.E.	Bachelor of Engineering
B.Ed.	Bachelor of Education
BENELUX	Belgium, Netherlands and Luxembourg countries
b/f	Brought forward (accounts)
bhp	Brake horse power
BIMARU	Bihar, Madhya Pradesh, Rajasthan, Uttar Pradesh states
B.L.	Bachelor of Law
B.Lit	Bachelor of Literature
B.Litt.	Bachelor of Letters
B.M.	Bachelor of Medicine
BO	Body odour
BOLT	Build Operate Lease Transfer
BP	Blood pressure
B.Phil.	Bachelor of Philosophy
Bro(s)	Brother(s)
B.S.	Bachelor of Surgery
B.Sc.	Bachelor of Science

****

C

C.	Celsius; centigrade
c.	(Latin *circa*) about
CA	Chartered accountant
cc	Cubic centimetre; carbon copy
CA	Chartered accountant
CAG	Comptroller and Auditor General of India
CAT Scan	Computerised Axial Tomography
CD	Compact disk
CEO	Chief executive officer
cf	(Latin *confer*) compare
c/f	Carried forward (accounts)
CFC	Chlorofluorocarbons (gases)
CID	Criminal Investigation Department
c.i.f.	Cost, insurance and freight
C-in-C	Commander-in-Chief

CII	Confederation of Indian Industries
CIS	Commonwealth of Independent States
C.J.	Chief Justice
CKD	Completely knocked down (kit)
cm	Centimetre
CMIE	Centre for Monitoring Indian Economy
CNN	Cable News Network
CNS	Central nervous system
C/o	Care of (in addressing letters)
CO	Commanding officer
COD	Cash on delivery
CPR	Cardio pulmonary resuscitation
CRR	Cash reserve ratio
CT Scan	Computerised tomography
CTBT	Comprehensive Test Ban Treaty (on nuclear weapons)
CV	Curriculum vitae
CVR	Cockpit voice recorder
Cwt	Hundredweight (112 lbs)
CYMK	**C**yan, **Y**ellow, **M**agenta, Blac**k**

****

D

D.A.	Dearness allowance
d.	Died
d.c.	Direct current (electricity)
DDT	Dichloro-diphenyl-trichloro-ethan (insecticide)
Dec.	December
DIY	Do it yourself
DJ	Disc jockey
D.Litt.	Doctor of Letters
DMZ	Demilitarised zone
DNA	Deoxyribonucleic acid (biology)
do.	Ditto, the same
D.Phil.	Doctor of Philosophy
DPT	Diphtheria, pertussis and tetanus (vaccine)

Dr.	Doctor
D.Sc.	Doctor of Science
DTP	Desktop publishing
DVD	Digital video disc

****

E

Email	Electronic mail
ECG	Electrocardiogram
EDI	Electronic data interchange
EDP	Electronic data processing
EEC	European Economic Community (the Common Market)
EEG	Electro encephalogram
e.g.	Latin *exempli gratia* (for example)
ELISA	Enzyme Linked Immuno Sorbent Assay (AIDS test)
ELT	English Learning and Teaching
EOU	Export oriented unit
EPABX	Electronic Private Automatic Branch Exchange
EPZ	Export processing zone
ESP	Extra sensory perception
EST	Eastern Standard Time (America)
et al.	et alii (and others)
etc.	Latin *et cetera* (and the rest); and so on

****

F

F	Fahrenheit
FAQ	Frequently asked questions
FII	Foreign institutional investors
FIR	First information report
FM	Frequency modulation (radio)
FMCG	Fast moving consumer goods
FYI	For your information
fwd	Forward

****

G

GATT	General Agreement on Tariffs and Trade
GDP	Gross domestic product
GDR	Global depository receipt
GI	General Issue (an American soldier); a private soldier
GIF	Graphics Interchange Format
GIS	Geographical Information System
GM	General manager
GMT	Greenwich Mean Time
GNP	Gross national product
G.P.	General practitioner (doctor)
GPO	General post office
GPS	Global positioning system

****

H

ha.	Hectare
H.E.	His (Her) Excellency
h.f.	High frequency (radio)
HIV	Human immunodeficiency virus
H.M.	Her (His) Majesty
HMS	Her (His) Majesty's Ship
HMV	His Master's Voice (music company); Heavy motor vehicle
Hon	Honourable; honorary
HP	Hire purchase
hp	Horse power
HQ	Headquarters
H.R.H.	Her (His) Royal Highness
HTML	Hyper text mark-up language
http	Hypertext transfer protocol
Hz	Hertz (unit of frequency)

****

I

ib., ibid.	Latin *ibidem* (in the same place)
i/c.	In charge
i.e.	id est (that is)
IAS	Indian Administrative Service
IBM	International Business Machines
ICBM	Inter-continental ballistic missile
ICJ	International Court of Justice
IFS	Indian Foreign Service; Indian Forest Service
IGNOU	Indira Gandhi National Open University
IIT	Indian Institute of Technology
ILO	International Labour Organisation
IMF	International Monetary Fund
Inc.	Incorporated (America)
Info	Information (informal)
Infra dig.	Latin *infra dignitatem* (beneath one's dignity)
I.N.R.I.	Latin *Iesus Nazarenus Rex Iudaeorum* (Jesus of Nazareth, King of the Jews)
INS	Indian Newspaper Society
INTERPOL	International Police
IOU	I owe you
IP	Internet protocol
IPC	Indian Penal Code
IPS	Indian Police Service; Inter Press Service
IQ	Intelligence quotient
IRBM	Intermediate range ballistic missile
IRC	International Red Cross
IRDP	Integrated Rural Development Programme
IRS	Indian Revenue Service
I.T.	Income tax
ISBN	International Standard Book Number
ISDN	Integrated Services Digital Network
ISI	Indian Standards Institute
ISKCON	International Society for Krishna Consciousness

ISO	International Standards Organisation
ISRO	Indian Space Research Organisation
IST	Indian Standard Time
ITBP	Indo-Tibetan Border Police
IUCD	Intra-uterine contraceptive device
IVF	In-vitro fertilisation

****

J

J	Joule (SI unit of work)
Jan	January
JCO	Junior Commissioned Officer
JP	Justice of Peace
JPEG	Joint photographic expert group
Jr	Junior

****

K

KG	Kindergarten
kg	Kilograms
kHz	Kilohertz
km	Kilometre
km/h	Kilometres per hour
K.O./k.o.	Knock-out (boxing)
KRC	Konkan Railway Corporation

****

L

Lab.	Laboratory
LASER	Light Amplification by Stimulated Emission of Radiation
LASIK	Laser in situ Kerato-mileusis
Lb	Latin *libra* (pounds, weight)
l.b.w.	Leg before wicket (cricket)
l.c.	Latin *loco citato* (in the place cited); lower case (printing)

LCA	Light combat aircraft
LCD	Liquid crystal display
LL.B.	Bachelor of Laws
LoC	Line of Control (on the Indian border)
LP	Long-playing (gramophone record)
LPG	Liquefied petroleum gas
LSD	Lysergic acid diethylamide (a drug)
LTA	Leave travel allowance
LTC	Leave travel concession
Lt	Lieutenant
Ltd	Limited (liability company)

****

M

MA	Magisiter Artium (Master of Arts)
Maj	Major
Max	Maximum
Mar	March
MBA	Master of Business Administration
MBBS	Bachelor of Medicine and Bachelor of Surgery
MC	Master of Ceremonies
MCP	male chauvinist pig (slang)
MD	Doctor of Medicine
M.Ed.	Master of Education
Messrs.	Plural of Mr [French *Messieurs*]
mfg.	Manufacturing
MFN	Most favoured nation (status)
mg	Milligrams
Mgr.	Monsignor; manager
Misc	Miscellaneous
MIT	Massachusetts Institute of Technology
MI	Military Intelligence (UK)
MI5	Counterespionage and internal security branch of MI (UK)
MI6	Secret Intelligence Service (UK, also called SIS)

min.	Minimum; minute
ml	Millilitre
MLA	Member of Legislative Assembly
Mlle	Mademoiselle (Miss)
Mme	Madame (Mrs)
MNC	Multinational Corporation
MO	Money order
MoD	Ministry of Defence
mod cons	Modern conveniences (informal)
MODEM	Modulator demodulator
MODVAT	Modified value added tax
MOU	Memorandum of Understanding
MP	Member of Parliament
MPEG	Motion Picture Experts' Group
mph	Miles per hour
Mr	Mister
MRCP	Member of the Royal College of Physicians
Mrs	Title used before the name of a married woman and short for Mistress
MRTPC	Monopolies and Restrictive Trade Practices Commission
Ms	Title used before Miss or Mrs (today considered the politically correct way of addressing a woman so as to not disclose her marital status)
M.Sc.	Master of Science
MS/MSS	Manuscript/manuscripts
Mt.	Mount
MTCR	Missile Technology Regime Control

****

N

NA	Not applicable, not available
NAFTA	North American Free Trade Agreement
NASA	National Aeronautics and Space Administration
NASDAQ	National Association of Software and Service Companies

NATO	North Atlantic Treaty Organisation
NAV	Net asset value
NB	Nota bene (note well)
NCAER	National Council of Applied Economic Research
NCC	National Cadet Corps
NCERT	National Council of Educational Research and Training
NCO	Non-commissioned officer
NDA	National Defence Academy; National Democratic Alliance
NE	North-east
NGO	Non-governmental organisation; non-gazetted officer
NIMHANS	National Institute of Mental Health and Neuro Sciences
n.o.	Not out (cricket)
no.	Italian *numero* (number) (plural *nos.*)
NOC	No objection certificate
Nov.	November
NPT	Nuclear Non-proliferation Treaty
NW	North-west
NY	New York (State)
NYC	New York City
NZ	New Zealand

****

O

OAU	Organisation of African Unity
Oct.	October
o/d	Overdrawn (banking)
OEM	Original equipment manufacturer
OGL	Open general licence
OIC	Organisation of Islamic Countries
OK	All correct (slang)
O-level	Ordinary level (educational)
OPEC	Organisation of Petroleum Exporting Countries
opp.	Opposite
OPV	Oral polio vaccine

ORT	Oral rehydration therapy
OTG	Oven-toaster-griller
oz	Ounce(s)

****

P

PA	Personal assistant
p.a.	Latin *per annum* (per year)
para	Paragraph
PAYE	Pay as you earn (income tax)
PC	Police constable; personal computer
pc	Per cent; postcard
PDA	Personal digital assistant (computers)
PEN	(International club of) Poets, Playwrights, Essayists, Editors and Novelists
PG	Paying guest
PJ	Poor joke
pH	A scale of acidity/alkalinity
Ph.D.	Doctor of Philosophy (Philosophiae Doctor)
PIB	Press Information Bureau
PIL	Public interest litigation
PIN	Postal index number
Pixel	Picture element
PM	Prime minister; post-mortem
p.m.	Latin *post meridiem* (after noon); per month
PO	Post office; postal order
POD	Pay on delivery (posts); proof of delivery (courier)
POW	Prisoner of war
pp	Pages
ppm	Parts per million (chemistry)
P.P.S.	Latin *post post scriptum* (a second postscript)
PR	Public relations
pro.	Professional
Prof.	Professor
pro tem.	Latin *pro tempore* (for the time being)

P.S.	Latin *post scriptum* (postscript)
PT	Physical training
PTA	Parent-Teacher Association
Pte.	Private (soldier)
P.T.O.	Please turn over
Pty	Proprietary (company)
PUC	Pollution under control (certificate)
PVA	Polyvinyl acetate (chemistry)
PVC	Polyvinyl chloride (chemistry)
PWD	Public Works Department

****

Q

Q	Queue; queen (chess)
QED	Latin *quod erat demonstrandum* (which had to be proved)
qt	Quart

****

R

RADAR	**Ra**dio **d**etection **a**nd **r**anging
RAM	Random access memory
RAW	Research & Analysis Wing
RC	Roman Catholic
RCC	Reinforced cement concrete
R&D	Research & Development
RDX	**R**esearch **d**evelopment e**x**plosive (a type of high intensity explosive)
recd	Received
REM	Rapid eye movement (sleep)
ref.	Reference; refer; referee
rep.	Representative
Retd.	Retired
Rev.	Reverend
r.f.	Radio frequency

Rh	Rhesus factor
R.I.P.	Latin *requiescat/requiescant in pace* (rest in peace), used on graves
RITES	Rail India Technical & Economic Services
Rly.	Railway
RMS	Railway Mail Service
RNA	Ribonucleic acid (biology)
ROM	Read only memory
rpm	Revolutions per minute
Rs	Rupees
RSPCA	Royal Society for the Prevention of Cruelty to Animals (UK)
RSS	Rashtriya Swayamsewak Sangh
RSVP	French *repondez s'il vous plait* (please reply, used at the end of invitations)
Rx	Prescription

****

S

SASE	Self-addressed stamped envelope
SE	South-east
Sept.	September
SF	Science fiction
Sgt.	Sergeant
SI	French *Systeme International* (International System – of units)
sic.	Latin *thus* (so written)
S&T	Science and Technology
SIDS	Sudden Infant Death Syndrome (crib deaths)
SKD	Semi-knocked down (kits for assembled products)
SLR	Statutory liquidity ratio (economy); single lens reflex (cameras)
SLV	Satellite launch vehicle
SMTP	Simple mail transfer protocol
SOHO	Small office home office

SOS	Radio signal for help (said to denote Save Our Souls), now *Mayday*
SPCA	Society for Prevention of Cruelty to Animals
sq.	Square
Sqn.	Squadron
St.	Saint; street; station
STD	Subscriber trunk dialling; sexually transmitted disease
stet	Latin *let it stand* (cancel the alteration)
Supt.	Superintendent
SWOT	Strengths, Weakness, Opportunities, Threats analysis (management)

****

T

TA	Travel allowance
TAM	Television audience measurement
TAAI	Travel Agents Association of India
TC	Ticket checker; ticket collector
T&D	Transmission & Distribution
TB	Tuberculosis
tbsp.	Tablespoon
tech.	Technology; technical
tel.	Telephone
temp.	Temperature; temporary
TIFF	Tagged Image File Format
TKO	Technical knockout (boxing)
TNT	Trinitrotoluene (an explosive substance)
TOEFL	Test of English as a foreign language
TQM	Total quality management
TRIPS	Trade Related Intellectual Property Rights
tsp.	Teaspoon
TTE	Travelling ticket examiner
TV	Television

****

U

UFO	Unidentified flying object
UGC	University Grants Commission
UHF	Ultra high frequency
UN	United Nations
UNCTAD	United Nations Conference on Trade and Development
UNEP	United Nations Environment Programme
UNESCO	United Nations Educational, Scientific and Cultural Organisation
UNFPA	United Nations Population Fund
UNI	United News of India
UNICEF	United Nations International Children's Emergency Fund (now United Nations Children's Fund)
UPS	Uninterrupted power supply
UPSC	Union Public Service Commission
URL	Uniform (or universal) resource locator (Internet address)
USAID	United States Agency for International Development
USP	Unique selling point
u-v	Ultra-violet

****

V

VAN	Virtual area network
VAT	Value added tax
VC	Vice chancellor; vice chairman; Victoria Cross
VCR	Videocassette recorder
VD	Venereal disease
VDIS	Voluntary Disclosure of Income Scheme
Vet.	Veterinary surgeon
VHF	Very high frequency (radio)
VHS	Video home system
VIP	Very important person
viz.	Latin *videlicet* (namely)

vol.	Volume
VPP	Value payable post
VSAT	Very small aperture terminal

****

W

WASP	White Anglo-Saxon Protestant (American)
WC/w.c.	Water closet (toilet)
WPI	Wholesale price index
WHO	World Health Organisation
w.p.m.	Words per minute
WTO	World Trade Organisation
WWF	Worldwide Fund for Nature
www	Worldwide Web
WYSIWYG	What you see is what you get

****

X

X	Roman numeral 10
X'mas	Christmas
XML	Extensible mark-up language
X-rated	Adult

****

Y

YMCA	Young Men's Christian Association
YWCA	Young Women's Christian Association

****

Z

ZIP	Zone improvement plan (US postal code)

∞

A Few Words About Words

There are reams of quotes on every topic under the sun. But few people have bothered to say a few words about words! Did you know that the most abused word is the word WORD? Consider all the radio spots and TV commercials where the announcer says, "And a word from our sponsor..." The WORD from the sponsor could then go on for the next ten seconds or ten minutes!

But what we present below are indeed just a few words on words...

A word is dead
When it is said,
    Some say.

I say it just
Begins to live
    That day.
  –Emily Dickinson

****

Words form the thread on which we string our experiences.

—Aldous Huxley

****

If God wanted us to speak more than listen, he would have given us two mouths and one ear.

—Mark Twain

****

Language is a Trojan horse by which the universe gets into the mind.
—Hugh Kenner, Canadian scholar and literary critic
*****

In human intercourse the tragedy begins not when there is misunderstanding about words, but when silence is not understood.
—Henry David Thoreau, American essayist and poet
*****

Silence is golden, but speech is silvern.

—Anonymous
*****

To travel anywhere in India, all you need to know are two words: 'How much?' and 'Too much!'

—Cynical American traveller

The Exploding World of SMS Words

SMS (Short Messaging Service) is a technology that permits users to send text messages of around 150 characters between mobile phones. SMS has fast developed as a language all its own, which youngsters enjoy using, while elders frown in disapproval. Since the messages have to be in minimal length and it is difficult to type on a phone keypad, SMS fans use a lot of abbreviations instead of full words. The common SMS words and sentences are presented in the following pages.

A

ADN	=	Any day now
@	=	At
8	=	Ate
A3	=	Anytime, anywhere, anyplace
AFK	=	Away from keyboard
ATK	=	At the keyboard
ASL	=	Age, sex, location
AFAIK	=	As far as I know
AFAIR	=	As far as I recall
ASAP	=	As soon as possible
ATB	=	All the best
ATM	=	At the moment
ASAP	=	As soon as possible
ATB	=	All the best

ATM	=	At the moment
Alwz	=	Always

****

B

B	=	Be
BCNU	=	Be seeing you
B4	=	Before
BBL	=	Be back later
BBS	=	Be back soon
BRB	=	Be right back
BRT	=	Be right there
BION	=	Believe it or not
BTDT	=	Been there, done that
BB	=	Bye-bye
B4N	=	Bye for now
BF	=	Boyfriend
BG	=	Big grin
BK	=	Big kiss
BAK	=	Back at keyboard
BOL	=	Best of luck
By	=	Busy
BTW	=	By the way
BFN/B4N	=	Bye for now
BS	=	Bullshit!
BTW	=	By the way

****

C

C	=	See/sea
CB	=	Call back
CID	=	Crying in disgrace
CSG	=	Chuckle, snigger, grin
CYR BOS	=	Call Your Boss
CYR BRO	=	Call your brother

CYR H	=	Call your husband
CYR M	=	Call your mother
CYR OFIS	=	Call your office
CYR FA	=	Call your father
CYR SIS	=	Call your sister
CYR WF	=	Call your wife
Cmon	=	Come on
Coz	=	Because
CUB l8r	=	Call you back later
Cum hre	=	Come here
CU	=	See you
CUL	=	See you later
CUL8R	=	See you later
C YA	=	See you
CWOT	=	Complete waste of time
CWYL	=	Chat with you later

****

D

D	=	The (affected pronunciation)
DK	=	Don't know
DNT	=	Do not
DUZ	=	Does
DUZNT	=	Does not
DNR	=	Dinner
Diff	=	Difference
DoN	=	Doing
DUR?	=	Do you remember

****

E

E2EG	=	Ear to ear grin
EOD	=	End of discussion
EOL	=	End of lecture

Evry1	=	Everyone
Ezy	=	Easy

****

F

4	=	For/four
4get	=	Forget
4N	=	Foreign
4e	=	Forever
FCOL	=	For crying out loud
F2F	=	Face to face
F2T	=	Free to talk
FITB	=	Fill in the blanks
FAQ	=	Frequently asked questions
FC	=	Fingers crossed
FOC	=	Free of charge
FOMCL	=	Fell out of my chair laughing
FWIW	=	For what it's worth
4YEO	=	For your eyes only
FYA	=	For your amusement
FYI	=	For your information

****

G

GAL	=	Get a life
GF	=	Girlfriend
GFN	=	Gone for now
GG	=	Good game
GTG	=	Got to go
GTH	=	Go to hell!
GMTA	=	Great minds think alike
GR8	=	Great!
Grr!	=	Angry
G9	=	Genius

GTSY	=	Glad/great to see you
GSOH	=	Good salary, own home
GUDLUK	=	Good luck

****

H

H2	=	How to
H2CUS	=	Hope to see you soon
HUH	=	Have you heard?
H8	=	Hate
HAGN	=	Have a good night
HAND	=	Have a nice day
HldMeCls	=	Hold me close
HHIS	=	Hanging head in shame
HHOK	=	Ha! Ha! Only kidding!
HHOS	=	Ha! Ha! Only serious!
HRU	=	How are you?
Ht4U	=	Hot for you
HTH	=	Hope that helps
H&K	=	Hugs and kisses

****

I

IAC	=	In any case
IAD8	=	It's a date
IC	=	I see
ICCL	=	I couldn't care less
ICQ	=	I seek you
IDK	=	I don't know
IK	=	I know
IIRC	=	If I recall correctly
ILU	=	I love you
IMBLuv	=	It must be love
IMI	=	I mean it
IMO	=	In my opinion

IMHO	=	In my honest/humble opinion
IN4ML	=	Informal
IOU	=	I owe you
IOW	=	In other words
IMTNG	=	I am in a meeting
IM4U	=	I am for you
Im:)2hvMtU	=	I'm happy to have met you
IRL	=	In real life
ITYS	=	I think you stink
ItsF8	=	It's fate
IUSS	=	If you say so
IWALU	=	I will always love you
IYD	=	In your dreams
IYKWIM	=	If you know what I mean

****

J

JK	=	Just kidding
J4F	=	Just for fun
JFK	=	Just for kicks
JstCllMe	=	Just call me
JMO	=	Just my opinion
JTLYK	=	Just to let you know

****

K

KC	=	Keep cool
KHUF	=	Know how you feel
KISS	=	Keep it simple, stupid
KNT	=	Cannot
KUTGW	=	Keep up the good work
KIT	=	Keep in touch
KOTC	=	Kiss on the cheek
KOTL	=	Kiss on the lips

****

L

L8	=	Late
L8R	=	Later
LHU	=	Lord help us
LMAO	=	Laugh my ass off
LOL	=	Laughing out loud
LMK	=	Let me know
LDR	=	Long-distance relationship
LTNS	=	Long time no see
Luv	=	Love
LUWAMH	=	Love you with all my heart
LtsGt2gthr	=	Let's get together
LY	=	Love you
LyN	=	Lying

****

M

MT	=	Empty
M8	=	Mate
MOF	=	Matter of fact
MTE	=	My thoughts exactly
MSULkeCrZ	=	Miss you like crazy!
MC	=	Merry Christmas!
MGB	=	May god bless
Mob	=	Mobile
MU	=	Miss you
MUSM	=	Miss you so much
MYOB	=	Mind your own business

****

N

NA	=	No access
NAGI	=	Not a good idea
NC	=	No comment

NE	=	Any
NE1	=	Anyone
NEthing2+	=	Anything to add?
Njoy	=	Enjoy
No1	=	No one
NP	=	No problem
NRG	=	Energy
NRN	=	No reply necessary
NWO	=	No way out

****

O

OIC	=	Oh, I see
OK	=	Okay
ONNA	=	Oh no, not again!
OMG	=	Oh my God!
OTT	=	Over the top
OTOH	=	On the other hand
O4U	=	Only for you

****

P

Pls	=	Please
PCM	=	Please call me
PDS	=	Please don't shout
PITA	=	Pain in the arse
Pl&	=	Planned
Plz4GVME	=	Please forgive me
Po$bl	=	Possible
PMFJI	=	Pardon me for jumping in
PPL	=	People
PRT	=	Party
PRW	=	Parents are watching
PTL	=	Praise the Lord
PTB	=	Please Text Back

PUKS	=	Pick Up Kids

****

Q

QPSA?	=	Que pasa? (What's happening?)
QT	=	Cutie

****

R

R	=	Are/Our
Re	=	Regarding
ROFL	=	Rolling on the floor laughing
RUOK	=	Are you okay?
Rgds	=	Regards
RINGL8	=	Running late
RLR	=	Earlier
RMB	=	Ring my bell
RTFM	=	Read the flaming manual
RU?	=	Are you?
RU CMNG?	=	Are you coming?

****

S

Sk8	=	Skate
SK	=	Sick
SOL	=	Sooner or later
Sry	=	Sorry
Spk	=	Speak
SYS	=	See you soon
SWAK	=	Sealed with a kiss
STATS	=	Your sex and age
ShopN	=	Shopping
Spk2UL8R	=	Speak to you later
SWG	=	Scientific wild guess

****

T

TAFN	=	That's all for now
TTFN	=	Ta-ta for now!
Txt	=	Text
Thx	=	Thanks
ThnQ	=	Thank you
T+	=	Think positive
2	=	To/too/two
2day	=	Today
2moro	=	Tomorrow
2nite	=	Tonight
2gether	=	Together
2g4u	=	Too good for you
2l8	=	Too late
2bctnd	=	To be continued
2d4	=	To die for
TDTU	=	Totally devoted to you
TIC	=	Tongue in cheek
TMIY	=	Take me I'm yours
TIA	=	Thanks in advance
TOY	=	Thinking of you
TTYL	=	Talk to you later
TTYT	=	Talk to you tomorrow
TUL	=	Tell you later

****

U

^	=	Up
U	=	You
U2	=	You too
UOK	=	You okay?
UR	=	You are/you're
Usu	=	Usually

UI!	=	You idiot!
URT1	=	You are the one
UR4Me	=	You are for me
U4E	=	Yours forever

****

V

VRI	=	Very

****

W

Wan2	=	Want to
WB	=	Welcome back
Wn	=	When
WTF	=	What the f—k!
WTG	=	Way to go!
WUF	=	Where are you from?
W8	=	Wait...
W84M	=	Wait for me
W4u	=	Waiting for you
Wot	=	What?
W/o	=	Without
1drfl	=	Wonderful
WFM	=	Works for me
W8N	=	Waiting
Wan2Ca moV?	=	Want to see a movie?
WRT	=	With respect to
WRU	=	Where are you?
WTH	=	What the hell!
WUWH	=	Wish you were here

****

X

Xlnt	=	Excellent
X	=	Kiss
Xclusvly Urs	=	Exclusively yours

****

Y

Y?	=	Why?
YBS	=	You'll be sorry
YM	=	You mean
YR	=	Your/Yeah, right!
YGM	=	You got mail

****

Z

Z	=	The (affected, as in "What's zee time?")
ZZZZZZZZZ	=	Sleeping

∞

www.ingramcontent.com/pod-product-compliance
Lightning Source LLC
Chambersburg PA
CBHW070309240426
43663CB00039BA/2506